T0157271

# A
# MORE
# EXCELLENT
# WAY

## MINISTER BILL

WESTBOW
PRESS®
A DIVISION OF THOMAS NELSON
& ZONDERVAN

WestBow Press books may be ordered through booksellers or by contacting:

WestBow Press
A Division of Thomas Nelson & Zondervan
1663 Liberty Drive
Bloomington, IN 47403
www.westbowpress.com
1 (866) 928-1240

ISBN: 978-1-9736-9809-8 (sc)
ISBN: 978-1-9736-9808-1 (e)

Print information available on the last page.

WestBow Press rev. date: 07/31/2020

# ABOUT THE AUTHOR

Minister Bill is the published author of Between the Lines and Live the Life. He has been a member of the same Baptist church for more than sixty-five years. He was ordained as a Minister of the Gospel in the year 2015. He has heard hundreds of sermons and he has read numerous books. He has come to the conclusion that pastors and preachers do not know anything. They go to school only to learn what others believe. Then they go to their churches to tell you what they believe. The fact is, you do not know anything. You only believe. Why do you believe in something for which you have no proof? You cannot even prove that there is a God. You have no proof because God does not want you to have any proof. God wants you to believe in Him beyond all explanation. You believe because you want to believe. You want to believe that there is a God of grace, love, and mercy. You want to believe that there is a home in glory for you after you leave this life. You believe in God because you want to believe in God.

Purpose of book: Inspiration of the Heart and Mind

# A MORE EXCELLENT WAY

There is faith, hope, and charity. The greatest of all is charity. Without hope there is no life. Faith opens up the possibilities for all things. How can anything be greater than faith in God? The greatest Commandment starts with the word love. The second greatest Commandment starts with the word love. God is telling us that above all He wants love to dominate our lives. He wants us to stop thinking about ourselves and think about charity to others. By following the second greatest Commandment, we are also following the first greatest Commandment. How can you hate one of God's children whom you have seen, yet, state that you love God whom you have never seen? There were people who hated Jesus because He was talking away their thunder. There are people who hate others because they do not look like they look. Is God color blind? No, God knew exactly what He was doing when He made you white or black female or male. Love thy neighbor as thy self. The Jews, during the times Jesus was here on earth, considered only other Jews their neighbors. Do you consider only people of the same financial status your neighbor? Do you consider only people with the same belief as your neighbor? The same color of skin? The only factor that will get you into heaven is love. You can have all the faith and hope that any human being can have and it will mean nothing without love. Love is inclusive. Caring about God's people without limitation. You might dislike the behavior of another person. However, it goes deeper than that. When we see another person fall who has done wrong, we rejoice. We call that justice. It might be justice but it is not love. We should pray that the Holy Spirit will come into that person's life and make a meaningful difference. Praying to God for the good and for the bad. Nothing can save this world. It is already lost. Most people are going to hell and there is nothing we can do about it. We can only help one person at a time through charity. LOVE. A More Excellent Way.

# IT IS ALL IN THE MIND

Seeing children in third world countries smile and laugh will make a person think about their own life. These children live a very hard life. They have never realized the advantages that some children have experienced. Yet, they smile. To these children, relationships are the most important factors. People who they love. Many do not know it, but, Jesus is living with them each and every day helping them to carry their loads. We can learn something from them. We don't take time to realize or appreciate how blessed we are. If we did, we would stop telling God how big our problems are and start telling our problems how big our God is. We would stop thinking about what we don't have and start giving God thanks for what we do have. We would face each day knowing that we are blessed because God loves us. Knowing that we can do all things through Christ who gives us strength. There would be no more low expectations. Our God is big. He is capable of carrying us to great heights. When we see a gate, it is not there to stop us. It is there for us to open and pass through to greater heights. When we see a bridge it is there for us to cross to the promised land. There will be many gates and bridges in our lives. They are not obstacles. They are opportunities. Nothing is too hard for our God. It is all in the mind. Life can be a wonderful experience when we live each day with God.

# THE WAR IS NOT OVER

We Christians seem to be in cruise control. We seem to think because Jesus died for the sins of all humanity the vast majority of the people of this world now praise His name. Such is not the case. The vast majority of people in this world do not believe in Jesus. 60% of the people in this world do not believe in Jesus Christ. Six out of every ten people you meet do not believe in Jesus or could not care less. There are 155 countries on the face of the earth. The people of 145 out of the 155 do not believe that Jesus Christ is the Son of God. Christianity is in the minority. The fight of Jesus, Peter, Paul and thousands of others is not over. It is the duty of Christians of this day to bring every soul possible to God through the Spirit of Jesus the Christ.

# JESUS

Christians believe in Jesus. Most Christians do not fully understand the Divine Nature of Jesus. Jesus was not created by God. God formed Jesus after His own imagine to do God's work. Jesus is the body of God Almighty. The mind and body of Jesus is God. The bible states that God said (let US create man after Our own imagine). The words US and OUR tells us that someone other than God was present. That someone was Jesus. Jesus was with God far before the creation of heaven and earth. Jesus formed the earth following the direction of God. The question has been asked, how were people Saved before Jesus? There were no people before Jesus. Jesus has always been at the right hand of God doing the work of God. The Old Testament was written four hundred years before the New Testament. Yet, the people of the Old Testament believed that God would send a Messiah to save the world. The Book of Isaiah states that a Messiah is coming from Galilee. Micah lived 500 years before the birth of Jesus into this world. Let he stated clearly that the Messiah would be born in Bethlehem and that He will be King of Kings and Lord of Lords.

We Christians of today must understand who Jesus really is. We must turn our backs on any writings that lessen the Divine Nature of Jesus the Christ. God gave us Jesus because He knew that we being human needed someone close to believe in. Someone who has walked this earth and been seen and touched by human hands. God, before Jesus, sent many prophets to tell His Word. Too often His Word fell on deaf ears. Because of the limitations of men, God sent His Son. The Word became flesh and made His dwelling among us. No one has ever seen God, but Jesus. Jesus has always been at the right hand of God.

# WHAT'S IT ALL ABOUT

You came into this world with nothing and you will leave with nothing. Some will leave sooner than others. Some will leave at birth. Others will last 100 years. Your chances of living a long healthy life are not good. There are more diseases than can be listed. Coronavirus, Ebola Virus, Cancer, HIV, Mumps, Malaria, Measles, Small Pox, Tuberculosis, Yellow Fever, Hepatitis, Diphtheria, Influenza. To name a few. There are other factors that could take you out. Killer Hornets,Tornado, Earthquake, Flood, Volcano, Hurricane, Wild Fire. People to include yourself. Suicide, Accident, Mass Murder, Terrorism. You don't stand a chance. You might as well accept it. You are going to live until you die and you don't know when that will be.

What's it all about? When I came into this world, someone else had to take care of me. If I live until old age, someone else will have to take care of me. There are a few years in between but they are short. Even shorter for some people. You better hurry up and enjoy them while you can because tomorrow was meant for some but tomorrow may never come. It all seems so senseless. There has to be more to it than this.

How did it all start? Nobody really knows. Who started it? Nobody really knows. Why am I here? Do I really know? I didn't have anything to do with coming here and I most likely will not have anything to do with leaving. I don't know. I can only believe. I might be right or I might be wrong. But there is nothing else for me to do but believe. I have been told that there is a God Who created all. They tell me this but they don't know. They only believe. They are only stating what they have heard. They say I have a spirit and a soul but they cannot prove it. They say that there is a Holy Spirit that will enter into my life and make me believe. They keep talking about the hereafter not the here and now. I'm no dummy. I realize that nothing here on earth is forever. Everyone dies. Everything dies. I have to work with what I have. I have nothing other than belief. Belief in something I cannot see or touch. But something I can feel. That's the only thing that makes any sense. Maybe that's what it is all about. Belief. Without Resurrection life is absurd. Without the promise of eternal life, life is about nothing. Jesus suffered and died to let us know why we live. We live for one primary purpose. Belief in God. There is no other answer.

This world has recently experienced a virus that has killed over two hundred thousand people in a time period of only four months. This lets people know that they control nothing on this earth. Their lives could end tomorrow. It is completely out of their hands. The coronavirus has only one positive. It brings people closer to God. It lets people know that eternal life with God is all that matters. We all are here on this earth for only primary reason. To praise God.

# PAID IN FULL

During the Christmas season my kids come by and we exchange gifts. Then they go back home to enjoy Christmas morning with their families. I normally spend Christmas Day by myself. One Christmas Day I went to Steak & Shake to get something to eat. There was a white lady in her sixties who I could tell was looking at me. When I looked her way, she continued to eat her food. When I looked up again, she was gone. When I finished, I asked the waiter for my bill. He told me that my ticket had been paid in full. I do not know why that lady decided to bless me. I had never seen her before and I would not know her if I saw her again. I do not know why Jesus decided to bless me. He didn't have to do it. He didn't have to go through such pain for me. Nails in His wrist and feet. Swore driven into His side. Why? Love. Love of His Heavenly Father and love for all of humanity. He washed away our sins. And now unto Him who is able to keep you from falling and present you faultless before His glories presents. We so often think of how we have lived our lives. We mentally punish ourselves for the wrongs that we have done and for that which we should have done but did not. Stop! Know that you are human and that you will sin. Know that Jesus paid the price for our sins of the past, present, and future. We have only to do right and be right. By doing so, we pay Jesus gratitude.

I once worked for a car rental company. One November day I decided to stop at a truck stop to eat lunch. This truck stop had good fresh salads for only $2.99. I made my selection and started to the cashier. A young black man in his late twenties took the salary out of my hands and told me to put my money away. I had never seen him before. I tried to tell him that I could make the payment. He gave the cashier full payment. He said Merry Christmas. Then he disappeared. Why me? Why did he pick me to bless? When the Holy Spirit is within you, it makes you do things without thinking. It does not matter what you look like. The Holy Spirit is within. The Holy Spirit was within Jesus. He knew that His sacrifice would bless the world.

When are we going to start living our lives in the beauty of holiness? Jesus has paid the price in full. It is finished. We only have to accept His blessings and praise His Holy Name.

# SLAVERY AND SKIN COLOR

Slavery had nothing to do with skin color. It had only to do with money. There are more differences in human beings than can be named. Slim-Fat, Tall-Short, Left Handed-Right Handed, White-Black, Fast-Slow, English-Spanish, Weak-Strong, Ugly-Cure, Big Feet-Small Feet, 20-20 Vision-Blind, Young-Old. Slavery was a way of getting rich. There are few businesses today that would not be successful if they had free labor. People saw the opportunity to make money by selling human beings. They had to find humans who were weak and could not defend themselves. They had to find people who were in plentifully supply. People who they could force to do their will. They found such people in Africa. Between 1700 and 1750 African slavery increased in American to over 31,000. White people were making lots of money off of black free forced labor. It just so happened that people in Africa were black. If they had been white, weak, and plentifully, they still would have been the subject of slavery. Force is the key word. Making another person do what you want done without great cost to you. Force is human nature. It has been a part of human life since the beginning of time. Read the bible. Israel held their own people as slaves. Israel was taken into slavery numerous times because they were physically weak and plentifully. Try to find one statement in the bible that condemns slavery. That is what this world is about Financial status. The rich and the poor. The effort to use other human beings for one's personal financial gain.

The color of one's skin was meaningless. It was simply the most distinguishable feature of the person. Slavery was replaced by ignorance. Even poor white's who had nothing to gain and who had never gained anything from slavery, used the color of a person's skin to make the statement I am better than you. Status. If you are white, you are right. If you are black, get back. I am entitled to the better job because I am white. I am entitled to higher pay because of the color of my skin. Force and status. No, I didn't have anything to do with being a white male. No, I didn't have anything to do with being physically stronger than a woman. It is correct that it has nothing to do with my merit. But I don't care. It puts me in a better position in this world and I'm taking advantage of it.

Status and force. Using force to better status. Empowerment is the only reason it is not more obvious in the United States today.

# HEAVENLY FATHER

We thank You for the blessings of this day. We thank you for permitting us strength of mind, body, and spirit to come into Your house this morning to praise Your Holy Name. Father we want the world to know that we love You, trust You, and have faith in You. That's what important. Our understanding of so many things might not be correct, but, our love, trust, and faith in You Father exceeds all understanding.

Father we have to stop keeping score. We seem to think that because we have done more good than bad in our lives that we have been Saved. We say to ourselves oh, I have repented by sins and I have tired to live my life in accordance to God's Will. Surely when God adds up the good and bad, He will judge me in good light. How wrong we are. We can't be good enough for a perfect God. Father You are not a score keeper. Sometimes we wonder Father why there is so much pain and suffering in this world. Maybe You are showing us Father that we are helpless without You. This world would turn us upside down without You Father. You don't want us to keep score. You want us to surrender all. You want us to lay our all on the alter. You want us to accept the fact that we are nothing without You. You want us to give our lives to YOU.

There are many Faiths in this world Father. All of them place the burden on the shoulders of each individuals to be Saved. All but one. Christianity is the only faith Father that has a Savior. Jesus has paid our debt in full. We have only to accept Him as our Savior and Lord. That's all we have to do. Give our lives to Jesus. He will take care of the rest. There is no pathway to heaven. We don't have to worry about getting to the other side of the Jordan. Jesus will pick us up and carry us to the other side of the Jordan. All we have to do is give our lives to Jesus. The Son of the living God.

Through the precious spirit of JESUS we pray. Amen.

# I WANT TO GET TO HEAVEN

Our destiny. We have been told that only by the Grace of God will we get to heaven. We have been told that our faith will have no determination. We have been told that our good deeds will have no determination. But, in the back of our minds we continue to believe that being a good person and doing more good than bad will help us in our efforts to be saved. It is difficult for us to think otherwise. Surely God did not give us the Ten Commandments only to disregard our efforts to keep them come judgement day. It is difficult to understand. What does God want? I have repented my sins. I have tried to live my life in accordance to the Will of God. What does God want of me? I'm trying to be as good as I know how.

We cannot be good enough to be worthy of a perfect God. God is not a score keeper. It is not difficult to understand. God wants us to surrender all. To lay our all on the alter. To give ourselves to Him. All other considerations are secondary. All other functions will follow without effort. Faith, good deeds, love will all be a part of our surrender. We will feel His peace. Things don't do me like they use to. Things don't seem to bother me like they use to. It's like fighting a war that I know I have already won. I know I will work through this problem because God is in control. Nothing can prosper against me because God is with me. I can do all things through God Who strengthen me.

# HOW DEEP IS YOUR FAITH?

Shadrach, Meshach, and Abednego were willing to die in a fiery furnace. Daniel was willing to die in a lion's den. Abraham was willing to sacrifice his beloved son Isaac upon the request of God. Jesus was willing to be suicided to save the Souls of God's people. How deep is your love in God? Would you give up the life of your child upon the request of God? Would you give up your life because you refuse to worship a god other than God Almighty? Would you be willing to die to save the Souls of others who you did not even know? Does your NO answer mean that your faith in God is weak, not all it should be? Should you have concerns? Will God still love and Save you with weak faith?

The important question is not the depth of your faith. It is the depth of the faith of God. God knows that you are weak. He knows that you will never be all you should be. He knew Peter was weak. Yet, the love that Jesus had for Peter never changed. Does God expect you to have the faith of Shadrach, Meshach Abednego, Abraham, Jesus? There is a difference between the faith of God and the faith of human beings. Regardless of how much you love God, your faith has limits. The reason for this is a lack of a positive imagination. God told Abraham that the world would be blessed through his off-springs. Abraham had trust and faith in God. He never viewed his son as being died. Abraham believed that God would put life back into the body of Isaac. Why is it that a parent will give up their life to protect a child, but, would not do the same to define their love for God? Do you love your Mother Father, wife, child more than you love God? Jesus said anyone who loves their Mother, Father, wife, child more than Me is not worthy of Me. Will you ever be worthy of God? Is it that you expect more of yourself than God expects of you? The fact is, you will never be worthy of God. You can give your all. All that you have and you will still never be worthy of God. You are not Abraham. You are not Jesus. My Grace is sufficient. This statement does mean in time of need. Salvation is a need.

Don't worry about being worthy of God. Thank God for His Grace. We will never be all that we want to be. If you can't fly, run. If you can't run, walk. But keep moving forward.

# BLACK JESUS

You might say it doesn't matter. The color or ethic group of an individual really doesn't matter. The fact is, it doesn't matter to God, but, it has always mattered to human beings. There are sound geographical and genetical reasons to believe that Jesus was a person of color. No, not having white skin with long blond hair. Jews, during the time of Jesus on this earth, where not white with blond hair. They were dark skinned Israelites. When we look at the descendants of Abraham, we recognize that the color Black was very much included. Shem, the forefather of Jesus, was black. One of the wives of King Solomon was black. The Moors were people of color. They ruled Europe until the Roman empire conquered them. The Moors gave praise to the black Jesus. When Rome took over, they changed black to white thus changing Europeans history and white washing black history.

There was a man name Josephus. A black Jew. A First Century writer who saw Jesus. He reported the description of Jesus as black skinned, short growth, eyebrows meeting, and an underdeveloped beard. When Alexander VI took over Europe, he hired men to destroy all pictures of Jesus. He also hired Leonardo de Vinci and Michelangelo to paint the image of Jesus to look like his son Cesare Borgia. Alexander VI made all people in the bible white deceiving the entire world.

Daniel had a dream. In his dream he saw a man that all human kind honored and bowed down to. He describes the man as having hair like pure wool. Read Daniel 7:9. We read the Book of Revelation. The Disciple John tells of the image of one with white hair like wool (Revelation 1:14). When is the last time you have seen a white man with hair like pure wool?

Let the truth be told. Why is it that blacks will praise a white Jesus, but, whites have a problem with the praise of a black Jesus? Does the color of His skin make Him any less the Messiah?

I am telling you this because I do not want you to get to heaven and have a second heart attack when you find that Jesus was a man of color.

Hate is a terrible thing. The Jews and Samaritans hated each other. For years, white people in the United States hated black people. White Christians in the South on Sunday morning would go to church to sing praises to God and Jesus. After church, they would go home to get their lawn chairs. They would go to the park to watch a black person hung from a tree. We must ask ourselves, would they have gone to church to praise Jesus if they knew He was black. Jesus saw a woman at the well. She was a Samaritan. Jesus befriended her and told her everything about herself. She ran to the village and told everyone. Many Samaritans then believed in Jesus.

Later Jesus attempted to enter a Samaritan village. They rejected Jesus. They knew he was the Messiah however their hate for Jews was stronger than their love for God. These people in the South, was their hate for black people greater than their love for Jesus?

Christianity is only what one wants it to be.

# THE GOD OF ISRAEL

The Israelites are and have always been one of the smallest classification of human beings on this earth. Why the Jew? The Jewish recording of history would have us to believe that the Jews where God's chosen people. Time and time again in the Old Testament we read the statement (the God of Israel). During those time there had to be millions of people in this world other than just the Jews. Are we to believe that none of these people, other than the Jews, believed in God Almighty? Where are their stories? Are we to believe that God turned His back on all the rest of the world and only gave His blessing to Israel? That is what scripture would have us to believe by stating THE GOD OF ISRAEL.

Why were the Jews chosen? Why not some others? Israelites where not chosen because of their faithfulness, bravery, or impressiveness. They have been shown to be some of the most unfaithful people on this earth. If we are to believe their claim to be God's chosen, it was an act of God's pure grace. God reserves the right to choose whomever he wants. I will have mercy on whom I will have mercy. This could mean that the Jews needed more of God's grace and mercy than others. Grace, receiving something you don't deserve. Mercy, not receiving something you do deserve.

God told Abraham, through your offspring ALL nations on earth will be blessed. From the beginning, God's purpose was to bless ALL of humanity. Every human being who would believe in Him. All nations. All races. From generation to generation God's love continues. From Jesus to Abraham to YOU.

# HOLY SPIRIT

When we are baptized, we are baptized in the name of the Father, Son, and the Holy Spirit. We want to be baptized because Jesus was baptized. We want to be baptized the way Jesus was baptized. Since Jesus is the Son, He could only be baptized in the name of the Father and the Holy Spirit. We know the Father, but, do we really know the Holy Spirit? Why is the Holy Spirit so important that it must be made a part of the Trinity?

There is no record of Jesus performing a miracle until He was thirty years old. There is no record of Jesus performing a miracle until He was baptized by John the Baptist. What happen to Jesus after His baptism? Scripture reads that the heavens were open unto Him and the Spirit of God descended upon Him. Scripture only tells us that there after Jesus performed His first miracle. Turning water into wine.

Jesus could perform no miracles until He was blessed by God with the Holy Spirit. At that time, until Jesus blessed His disciples with the Holy Spirit, no one else on the face of the earth possessed the Holy Spirit. Jesus said numerous times that He could do nothing on His own. He was empowered by the Holy Spirit. The Will of God.

The whole life of Jesus on earth was empowered by the Holy Spirit – the Will of God. That is how much Jesus needed the Holy Spirit. Since the Holy Spirit was needed to this degree by Jesus, that tells us how much the Holy Spirit is needed by us. We are nothing without God. God directs our lives each and everyday through the Holy Spirit. God's Holy Spirit is with us twenty-four hours a day. Yes, even when we sleep. Caring for us. Loving us. God so loved the world that He gave us the life of His only begotten Son to save our souls. God is love. Free from sin. Free at last, free at last, Thank God Almighty I'm Free at LAST.

# ABRAHAM DESCENDANTS

Why is it that Muslims and Jews hate each other and continue to fight each other? We must understand that there were numerous ethic groups of people on the earth during Old and New Testament years. When reading the Old Testament, we read numerous times where God is referred to as the God of Israel. Are we to believe that no other ethic group on the face of the earth believed in God Almighty? Or, are we to believe that God turned His back on all of civilization and gave His blessing only to Israel? Where are the writings of other ethic groups during these times?

We wonder why the Roman Catholic bible has 80 books while the Hebrew bible only has 66. Why were the 14 books included in King James 1611 not included in the Hebrew bible? The reason is that the people who made the decision as to the writings to be in the Hebrew bible decided that these 14-books were spurious meaning bogus, false, deceitful. Greek-speaking Jews included these books known as apocryphaor/deuterocanonical. Present day Christians will never know the true complete story of the Old Testament. We are reading what others want us to read.

God told Abraham that He would be made a great nation through his descendants. Abraham had numerous children and grandchildren. Both Jews and Arabs believe they are descendants of Abraham. Jews state that they are descendants because of Isaac and Jacob. Arabs believe they are descendants because of Ishmael and Esau. They believe that because Ishmael and Esau were first born, not Isaac and Jacob, Arabs are closer to Abraham than Jews. Christians believe they are descendants of Abraham by faith. Spiritual adoption.

There were numerous ethic groups during the Old and New Testament years to include Samaritans, Greeks, Romans, and Barbarians. When will Jews and Arabs understand that if they truly love God they will find a way to love each other?

# ABUNDENT LIFE

God wants His children to live an abundant life. What is an abundant life? It certainly could not include physical welfare. There are too many cases of human pain and suffering for this to be the case. We must therefore conclude that abundant living has nothing or very little to do with our physical state. All that is remaining is our minds. It's all in the mind. We every day witness people who have mental difficulties. People who spend their lives hurting others. People who have no patience with others. Some people do unwise things. They do these things without thinking about the consequences. Of primary importance is living life thinking about consequences. Sometimes we find ourselves in the wilderness. Sometimes it is our fault because we did not think about the consequences. Sometimes it is the fault of others. God has told us that His grace is strongest when we are in the most need. When we can do very little for ourselves. When we have to depend solely on God. The wilderness draws us closer to God. This makes us stronger. We learn at a very early age that this life must come to an end. Yet, we continue to function as if we will live forever. We don't want to face reality. We don't want to face the fact that something put us here on earth and has granted us a limited amount of time to fulfill our purpose. So, we continue to live not accepting the fact that tomorrow was meant for some, but, tomorrow may never come.

A rich plentiful supply of love, peace and joy. It has been said that nothing good comes without sacrifice. We must submit to the lack of importance of this life. This life is nothing more than a gateway to heaven. That is the reason it is limited. When your Heavenly Father determines that you are ready, or that you will never be ready, to enter His Kingdom, He will end your life. It has nothing to do with your physical struggles. A person confined to a bed or wheelchair the remainder of life can have love, peace and joy. It is all in the mind and heart. The sacrifice we must make to live an abundant life is control. We must give-up control of our lives. We must be willing to accept Jesus as a young child accepts a parent. Jesus told us that only when we become as a little child will we be acceptable into God's Kingdom. We must become as sheep knowing and obeying the voice of our shepherd Jesus. No other voice can we recognize or follow. It was not designed to be easy. Getting into heaven is not easy.

To live an abundant life, we must obey the laws of the Lord. God's abundance is available to us only when we live life under God's government. There is a government of this society, but, we must give to Caesar that which is Caesar's and to God the things that are God's. God will be patient with us. However, we should never confuse His patience with His final decision. There is a very narrow door leading to heaven. Nothing that good can come with ease. We must live our lives with the primary goal of getting through that narrow door. There are rewards in this life for doing so. But, the difficulty level is very high. Most people will not make it. It is not all their fault. It is natural for human beings to think first about themselves. Being a natural human being will not get you to heaven. We must believe that even when the body die we have an inheritance reserved in heaven.

We must have a strong unwavering assurance of eternal life. We must not only believe that heaven is our final dwelling place, but, we must live like we believe. That is too hard to do for most human beings because self-interest, not God, controls their lives. We are intelligent people. We know that this life is only temporary. Yet, we continually give material things a place in our lives above that which is eternal. Maybe we are not so smart after all.

We wonder what God is waiting for. You want a life of love, peace and joy. You have gotten down on your knees and asked God to take it away. Anything within you that is keeping you from the joy that is yours, take it away. God is waiting on you. He wants to fill your tank with the riches of this life, but, your tank is already full. Filled with anxiety, selfishness, self-dependence, unforgiveness, anger to name a few. There is no room for God's treasurers. God is waiting on you to empty your tank of all negative factors so that He can fill you up with His abundant blessings.

Too often we think of God only when we feel we need Him. We dwell on the present. We forget the party that made things good. Or, is it that we do not believe it is He who is the reason for the good times? This most certainly could not be the case since we come crawling back during difficult times of guilt and grief. This situation will not happen if we have accepted God in the right spirit. When we develop to the point that we make God the director of our lives, all ungratefulness will disappear. We will praise God for who He is and not for just what He can do for us. We will praise God in the good times and the bad times because we understand that He is the controller of all. That's a part of cleaning out your tank. Getting rid of all the selfishness, ungratefulness, and self-dependence. Making room for that which is abundantly good.

We can only have an abundant life when we have a total commitment to God. We must have an intimate relationship with the Lord before the blessings of an abundant life are possible. First and far most God wants your heart. Your heart controls your head and your head will control your actions. We do not have to be concerned about service. Service will come automatically when your heart belongs to God. It is no longer necessary to think about what is right and what is wrong. When your heart belongs to God, your heart will do the thinking for you. Total commitment means total trust in the decision-making powers of the Almighty.

We search for the spirit of God so that we might have an abundant life. We pray, go to church, sing pretty songs of praise. We dig deep to find the mystery that remains hidden from all sources we exploit. It's not there. We are looking for that mysterious spirit in all the wrong places. We are searching for a spirit that is already deep within us. I will put My spirit within you and cause you to walk in My ways. It is hidden within. God is good at hiding that which is most valuable. God hid baby Moses from Pharaoh the ruler of Egypt. God hid baby

Jesus from King Herod. That which is most valuable to God is hidden. God requires sacrifice to find and employ these gifts in service to Him. Nothing this valuable will be found on the surface. You must dig deep within. Scripture tell us that if we seek the Lord with all our heart and soul, we will find Him.

Nobody said the road would be easy. It's difficult. Living a life that is pleasing to Almighty God is difficult. So difficult that most people will not stay the course. They get on the right road and find out that there are pot holes, mountains, and even snakes in their path. So, they start making excuses for not staying the course. One popular excuse is thinking that God is only using them to bring someone else His way. Once God has used me up, He will push me aside and final someone else. How wrong they are. God wants you much more than He wants anything you can do for Him.

God loves you for who you are not for what you can do for Him. Above all, God wants a relationship with you. An intimate relationship. No one else in this world is more important to God than you. Staying the course is the most difficult part of God's plan.

Anybody can fight a good fight for a short period of time. Only those who want an abundant life (good) enough will go through hades for a heavenly cause. Personally, I would rather live in His world than live without Him in mine.

# TRANSFORMATION

There are many Christians who want to be transformed into a living sacrifice to and for God. Jesus told us to not conform to this world, but, be transformed by the power of His word to become a living sacrifice. This is what we must want for our lives. There is no force applied by the Almighty. We must take the first step. Too often we pray asking God to do for us that which we will not put forth effort to help do for ourselves. We seem to think that all of the weight and responsibility is on God and we only have to wait. Oh, God will make a way somehow. Scripture reads wait on the Lord. So, I'm just going to sit here and wait. You have it all wrong. All prayer and no work won't work. The gospel tells us to knock and the door will be open. Seek and we shall find. The door will not be open unless we knock. We will not find that which we are looking for until we seek. We must start the process.

We start the process by the renewal of the mind. We must know and understand the word of God. No, you cannot believe everything you hear or read. You must first understand and believe that God loves you. No one who really loves you will ever tell you to do anything that will hurt you or hurt another. There are numerous false teachers who will deliver the wrong message. Believe in Almighty God and no one else. Knowing the word of God cannot be stressed enough. Only your knowledge will keep you on the right path. Your knowledge of and your belief in God.

This is a very deep well. We love and support God and Jesus Christ because we know what is inside. Love, compassion, mercy, peace, grace. Do not conform to this world. When we truly believe this, we will not conform or support anyone not having these same qualities. We will not support a person with no moral fiber as has over seventy-percent of Evangelical Protestant Christians have done. We will first look at the kind of moral fiber that person has. We will not give that person our support simply because that person will do that which we want done. No, not if we are true to the word of God. The character of a person, deep within, is that person. When we permit that which we want to take priority over the word of God, we have deep within committed a sinful act.

All Christians need transformation. We are living in a sinful world. You will be able to survive and do the will of God only when you deep within truly transform your mind and offer your life as a living sacrifice to God.

# FOLLOWERS OF JESUS

There are some very important points of understanding that we must accept if we are to be true followers of Jesus Christ. First, there is nothing more important than the Spirit of God. The Holy Spirit is the Spirit of God. You can insult almost anything but the Holy Spirit. For insulting the Holy Spirit, you will never be forgiven. You will condemn yourself to eternal damnation. Secondly, we must understand why we follow Jesus. Many people followed Jesus in massive numbers when He walked this earth. They were more concerned with their physical state than their spiritual state. They were more concerned with being healed physically. They did not understand that the primary reason Jesus came to them was to heal their hearts and to save their souls. Third, followers of Jesus must stop putting the weight of their Salvation only on Jesus. To wait on the Lord does not leave us without responsibilities. All prayer and no work just does not work. When we work, we must trust God's leadership. The judgment of God is great. Remember, experts made the titanic. Amateurs made the ark. Jesus will direct your path, but, you have to walk it. Knock and the door will be open. God has put His Spirit deep within you. You have to find it. Fourth, followers of Jesus must not wait until the need is too great for them to handle before seeking the help of the Lord. A little bit of Jesus applied to a big mess just does not work. Prayer without faith is just wishful thinking. No decision can be completely correct without the input of the Holy Spirit. Fifth, stop trying to impress God. We are not saved because we follow the Commandments. We follow the Commandments because we are saved. Last, God is love. The greatest thing you will ever learn is just to love and be loved in return.

# RELIGION

'm so glad I got my religion in time. Are you really? You don't know anything. You only believe. Belief is a powerful word. There are numerous religions in this world. Some believe in a god and some who don't. Christianity, Hinduism, Islam, Judaism. There is also a religion unique to a single country like Shinto in Japan. How do you know that your religion is the right one when all of these people believe something different? Then there are those who claim to believe in God but put their own twist into the mix like the Pharisees. Then there are those who claim to believe in God but do not believe in Resurrection like the Sadducees. Then there are those who do not believe at all. Buddhism is not a religion. It is a belief of Eastern Asia that teaches the value of meditation not belief in a Creator. Judaism is a Jewish religion that believes in the Old Testament of the bible, but, does not put much stock in the New Testament. Christianity is the largest religion with over two billion followers, however, even Christianity has more divisions than you can count. Baptist, Methodist, Presbyterian, Catholic, Lutheran. The list goes on and on.

Yes, religion in this world is a big mess. I'm right and everybody else in this world is wrong. The fact is that you do not know that you are right. You believe but you do not know and you will never know during this life. You believe in the cause, nature, and purpose of life. You believe that there is nothing more important than your spiritual life. Chances are you are a Christian who believes in the Old and New Testaments. Testimonies written by Jews and Jews alone. Do you really believe that God turned His back on all the other ethic groups on the face of the earth and administered only to the Jews during the time period as stated in the bible? Where are all the other testimonies of people who lived during this time period? We often wonder why God selected the Israelites to be His chosen people. That's what Jewish people will tell you. We must first understand the will, plan and timing of God. If you are a Christian, you must understand that the will, plan and timing of God was determined even before the selection of Abraham. The will of God was the life, death, and Resurrection of Jesus Christ to make the statement to all of humanity of the love of God. That's all that really counts. The love of God. Because of His love, we should love Him with all our heart soul, mind, and strength. We don't have to get caught up in religion to do that. Religion is a return to bondage. Feel free to love God regardless of your religious beliefs. We Christians will always love and believe in Jesus. Why? Because of our love of God.

# HEALING

When we read the New Testament, we are told of the numerous physical healing acts of Jesus. We are told of the multitudes of people who followed Him and we are told of His teachings. More attention seems to be given to the physical healing powers and the results thereof than spiritual healing and results. Human beings are mentally weak. They are attracted by the physical much more than the spiritual. The multitudes of followers were first and far most attracted to Jesus because of His physical healing powers. Yet, the primary reason for the earthly existence of Jesus was spiritual. Jesus came to us to save our Souls. To provide a way and means for us to overcome the only factor that keeps us separated for God that being sin.

Sin destroys our character. Sin makes us suffer through acts of violence, hatred, jealousy, and conflict. Sin destroys our minds making them corrupt, twisted, and perverted. Because of sin we will never be what we could and should be. We will never be as close to God as we ought to be.

Jesus knew all of these things. He knew that only through His ultimate suffice would human kind have the opportunity for eternal life. Isaiah 53:5, "But he was wounded for our transgressions, he was bruised for our iniquities: the chastisement of our peace was upon him; and with his stripes we are healed." The suffice of Jesus healed our character from the spiritual damage of sin.

Our physical state is not important. We can suffer through all of our physical pain. Regardless of how much we suffer, we will never experience the level by which Jesus suffered for us so that we may have eternal life.

# PRAYER

I t's a no brainer. Your head being involved in prayer can get you into trouble. When you pray, you think too much. All kind of trash is going through your head. You don't have to think about God. You know Him well. You don't think about the goodness of your parents. You simply accept them for who they are. They have proven themselves time and time again as has God. Your love of God is the reason you pray. Love comes from the heart. For of the abundance of the heart his mouth speaketh. We have heard the phrase speaking in tongue. That sometimes happens when the Holy Spirit takes control of your heart and mouth. You will say things you have never said before. The Spirit of God has taken control of your being. This might happen during a private or public prayer. Often times we hear people say that they cannot offer a public prayer. That is because they are praying with their minds not their hearts. Your heart controls your mind and your mind control your actions. As Jesus told His disciples, don't worry about what you will say. The Holy Spirit will put the words in your mouth when you are praying from your heart.

Sometime we become upset when we feel God is not answering our prayers. There are numerous reasons. One of the primary reasons is timing. You want your prayer answered when you want it answered. When is the last time you have prayed and ask God to treat you any kind of a way? Every time you pray, you make a special request. If you will accept anything on the menu, your prayer might get faster results. Special orders take time. God knows your situation better than you. His timing is always perfect. Trusting the correctness of His answer and His timing is important.

No, it does not have to only be on Pentecost God's Holy Day. It can be any day at any time of the day or night. Whenever you give your heart completely to God. The Holy Spirit will fill your heart with the love of God. It's a wonderful feeling. We worship a wonderful God.

# HEAVEN II

Heaven is our goal. We know that we will only be here a short period of time. We might not act like it, but, we know it. Everyone wants to go to heaven, but, not right now. The reason is that we do not exactly know what it will be like. There are so many questions that will never be answered in this life. We can only trust in the goodness of God. The pure in heart will see God. A pure heart is not easy to attain. Our hearts must be pure toward everyone not just the people we love. We must ask God with a pure heart for forgiveness of our sins. There are many who believe that sins are automatically forgiven because of the actions of Jesus. Scripture tells us that if we do not repent we will parish. We so badly want to see Jesus. We are told that while on earth He looked just like anyone else. We have also been told that He had dark skin and hair like pure wool. People with pure hearts do not care about the personal appearance of Jesus. We care only about His actions and that which came out of His mouth. Most people in this world do not believe in Him. We don't know if they will get to heaven. That's Jesus call.

Scripture tells us that the pure in heart will see God. This tells us that we will have a sense of recognition when we get to heaven. Luke 13:28 reads "…Ye shall see Abraham, Isaac, Jacob all the prophets, in the kingdom of God…". Yes, we will again see our earthly love ones. What an awesome God we serve.

We must set our priorities. We cannot listen to those who are not of full understanding. The opinions of others must never have the weight of our belief and trust in God. We must question our priorities. We love mother, father, children, sister, brother. How deep is your love? Does your love for your family take priority over your love for God? You must understand that you will one day lose that person. That person was not first yours. That person first belonged to God. Your feeling for that person should be secondary to your love of God.

Salvation is free, but, it is not without cost. Freedom is free, but, it is not without sacrifice. You want to go to heaven. It is going to cost you something. For many, it cost too much. You have to take up the Cross of Jesus everyday of your life. You can't do that which you want to do. God has told you in detail how you should live your life. Detail. Just going to church on Sunday morning will not get you to heaven. It takes a seven day a week commitment. Jesus told you exactly what is expected of you. Fulfilling some of His commands is not good enough. You must work to be perfect just as your Father in heaven is perfect. No body said the road would be easy. You must keep God in the back of your mind twenty-four hours a day. You can do this when you believe that you are a winner. You are a winner in this life and in death because God has saved you and prepared a better place for you in heaven.

Thank God for His many blessings. For life itself. The air you daily intake. The food you daily intake. His blessings are all around you. His primary blessing is the knowledge and wisdom that He has given to you. The wisdom of the glory of God. Give God the glory for the things He has done.

# HUMILITY

Who do you think you are mister big stuff? You're never going to get my love. You pray yet things are not working out for you. You are at a cross-road not knowing which way to go or how to get there. Your life is not all you would like it to be and you simply don't know how to make it better. Consider this. Humility. Maybe you are thinking more about that which you want than you are about how to get there. You believe in God, but, do you believe in Him more than you believe in yourself? What really does lay your all on the alter mean? Why are you holding back? It is time for you to accept the belief that as long as you hold back your commitment to God, He will hold back your blessings. We have to accept that which God has offered us now if we desire a tomorrow. Luke 16:31 "… If they hear not Moses and the prophets, neither will they be persuaded, though one rose from the dead." We must believe in the teaching of Jesus during His life here on earth or neither will they be persuaded, through one rose from the dead. Not only must we believe, we must live like we believe. We must be faithful to God not to mammon. No servant can serve two masters, for either he will hate the one, and love the other, or else he will hold to the one, and despise the other. Ye cannot serve God and mammon. Jesus has told us exactly what we must do. He who would be first must be last. He who shall be the greatest in heaven shall be the servant of all here on earth. Jesus did not come to be ministered to, but to minister to all those in need.

You want improvement in your life. Stop thinking about yourself. Think about God. Think about His goodness. Think about His grace that has brought you this far and has the power to take you higher. Direct your attention to the Almighty. Praise His name. I Am, that I Am. He will take you to heights you have never dreamed of. You can do all things through Christ Who strengthens you. Give God the glory and He will direct your path.

# JUDGMENT

The judgement of Jesus will determine our path after this life. It is not an easy determination to understand. The decision of Jesus is very important to us. He has told us that the pure in heart shall see God. We have been told that Jesus has washed away our sins past, present, and future. We have been given numerous Commandments to follow. Are we to believe that our level of obedience will have no effect upon the judgement of Jesus? We have been told that our earthly actions will have no measure in regards to the grace of God. Yet, we have been told that we serve a just God and He will not forget our kindness to His children. We have been told that we will not enter into the Kingdom of God if we have not been born again. We have been told that we have already witness judgement day when we accepted Jesus Christ as our Lord and Savior. Why is it so complicated? We believe in the bible. We know that the bible is an expression of the opinions of others, but, we want to believe in it. Or, should we believe in God, Jesus, and the Holy Ghost since only they have never been subject to the bias of mankind? Let's be truthful about it. We have been told so many things that we don't know what to believe.

You see, man will not tell us the truth the whole truth and nothing but the truth. One reason is pride. Have you ever heard a person of the Jewish faith tell you that Jews caused the death of Jesus? Pride has and will destroy the truth. Nowhere in the bible will the appearance of Jesus be told. Is the reason pride? Another reason we will not be told the whole truth is because it is unknown. So, we are left with opinions. Opinions of bias self-centered human beings who express what they believe yet do not know. That's the beauty of it all. No one can prove you wrong. Believe it or not, God wants it that way. The bible begins stating that in the beginning God created the heaves and the earth. The bible makes no attempt to prove that there is a God. God knew what was in man. God wants us to believe in Him without reservation. Without proof. Believe in Him so much that we will live our lives in accordance to His word.

That's all that is necessary. Give your life to God and live like it. You don't have any control over the judgment of Jesus Christ so stop worrying about it. Yes, you want to see God, Jesus, and your love ones in paradise. Your heart and your actions will play a big part in your wishes materializing. Trust in the goodness of God. He has never made a mistake.

# A GIFT FROM GOD

Your gift is your destiny. God has given each of us a special gift. Too often we do not realize the value of this gift. This gift is the riches of God's glory in you. With it, you are able to find your purpose in life. Too often we do not realize God's blessings. Too often we do not recognize the help we are receiving from Jesus in our everyday lives. We began to take Jesus for granted. This can be a serious mistake. God wants to know that you appreciate Him. Your love ones want to know that you appreciate them. When is the last time you have told a close relative that you appreciate them? When is the last time you have told God that you appreciate Him? Why do we pray? God already knows what we need and want. He will make it available when the time is right if it is best for you. So why pray? The main reason for prayer is praise. Father, You are appreciated. Above all, I give You the glory for the things You have done.

God lets us know things without us realizing it. It did not just start with us. More than five hundred years before the birth of Christ into this world there were many prophecies of the coming of the Messiah. The Old Testament reveals hundreds of details telling of the coming of the Messiah. That He will be born of a virgin woman, place, Son of God, rejected by His own people the Jews, betrayed, hated without cause, crucified with criminals, none of His bones would be broken, Resurrection, His sacrifice for the sins of humankind. How could all of these prophecies materialize hundreds of years before the birth of Jesus? There can be only be one answer. A gift from God. The bible was created for only one primary reason. Jesus. From Genesis through Revelation and 400 years in-between, Jesus was the reason. The Old Testament telling of the many miracles of God to prepare us for the miracle of Jesus.

God is full of miracles. You are a miracle. You are a gift from God. Think about your body and how all the different parts work together. Think about your mind how complicated it is. Think about the un-limitations of the human brain. Think about the wisdom given to you by your Heavenly Father. Wisdom to accept Him as your divine Master and Creator of the universe. The greatest thing you will ever learn is to love God and accept the love of God into your life.

# THE WORD MADE FLESH

The word was made flesh and dwelt among us. By reading this, we think that by believing in Jesus Christ we will believe in God. For some this is a difficult realization, but, the purpose of Jesus was first to reveal the glory, grace, and power of God. Jesus said, my doctrine is not mine, but His that sent Me. Jesus was dependent upon the Holy Spirit. The Spirit of God. Jesus stated numerous times that He could do nothing within Himself. All done was through the power of God given to Him by the Holy Spirit. We believe in Jesus. We believe in the bible. Both are important to us. They both exist because of God. Everything exist only because of God. Jesus is worthy of our praise. We worship only God. The purpose of Jesus is to strengthen our belief and relationship in and with God. The purpose of the bible is to strengthen our belief and relationship in and with God. Reading the bible will not make a person a Christian. The miracles of Jesus did not turn people into true believers. There had to be the understanding that the miracles of Jesus came from God. Jesus told us that no man can come unto Him, except it were given to him of the Father. A person must first be injected with the Holy Spirit before believing in Jesus or the bible. We do not realize the power of the Holy Spirit. The Spirit of God. Jesus has told us that a human can cast down anything and still be forgiven. All but the Holy Spirit. One who cast down the Holy Spirit will never be forgiven. One who cast down the Spirit of God will never be forgiven.

Jesus came to us to let us know that the spirit of God is within us. Trouble don't last always. Trouble can be all around you, but as long as it is not in you, you can last the storm. This is the reason Jesus used the statement, oh yea of little faith. The storm will tell what you are made of. The real revelation will come after the storm. When the spirit of God is within you, you will make that which you have left after the storm productive. You don't have to keep running to God for help. His spirit is already within you. All you have to do is use it. You can do all things through Christ who has given you strength. What is in you is all that counts. Your soul has been anchored in the Lord.

Learning about God is not easy. So often we hear but we do not fully understand. You hear the message with your ears but the true meaning of the message has not yet been planted in your heart, soul, and character. It takes time to grow in the spirit of God. A strong foundation must be constructed upon which to build. The higher the building the deeper must be the foundation. Often, hard times are building blocks to a strong foundation. Trusting God during hard times will make you grow in God's spirit. It's not easy to wait on the Lord. We need to listen for His voice. For His direction. If you don't hear anything, maybe it's because the power is not connected. You can turn on the radio many times, but if you do not have it plugged into the electrical outlet you will not hear anything. The electrical outlet is Jesus. Only through Him can you be connected to God. Jesus has told us that no one comes to the Father but by Him. God has a world of responsibility. His helper is Jesus. God has granted Jesus the responsibility, power and glory to help us whenever we are in need. We must pay the bill if we what the power to be given to us when we make the connection. Your heart must be righteous and true. You must have made every attempt to live to the glory of God. Just lip service does not get it. Faith without action is not true faith. The Word made Flesh. Jesus walked this earth just like you. He faced the same trials and tribulations as you now face. People were trying to kill Him from the day He was born.

They were unsuccessful because it was not the will of God. Making the necessary connection will only be there if you are true to God in your heart, mind, and actions.

Jesus told of the Comforter. Jesus knew that He could only be with us for a short period of time. His purpose was to tell us of the love, grace, mercy, and power of God. His primary purpose might have been to bring to us a source that would be with us forever. The Comforter. The Holy Spirit. The Spirit of God. But the Comforter, which is the Holy Ghost, whom the Father will send in my name, he shall teach you all things, and bring all things to your remembrance, whatsoever I have said unto you. This was too important to depend only upon writings of men. There are too many Judas Iscariot in this world. Too many who have the spirit of Satan within them. Those who will lead you away from Christ. Those who will prevent you from finding Christ. Remember the word that I said unto you. All these things will they do unto you for my name's sake, because they know not Him that sent Me. But when the Comforter is come from the Father, the Spirit of Truth will be with you forever. This joy I have. The world didn't give it and the world can't take it away. The Spirit of God within you.

We celebrate Christmas, the birth of Jesus into this world. How deeply do you believe in Jesus? Do you really understand the Divine nature of Jesus Christ? The word made flesh. Flesh did not exist before the Creator. Flesh did not exist before Jesus the Son of God. I have finished the work which thou gave Me to do. And now, O Father, glorify thou Me with Thine own self with the glory which I had with thee before the world was. Jesus the Christ was at the right hand of God Almighty before the creation of the world. Scripture tells us that God loved Jesus before the foundation of the world. It is impossible for Jesus to ever question the faith that His Father had in Him. Impossible. You could never question the love of your mother. Never question the Divine nature of Jesus the Christ.

The Word made flesh. Yet, His own people, the Jews, would not believe in Him. The world hated Him for no just reason. The vast majority of this world still does not believe in Jesus. The vast majority of this world are not children of God. There is a misconception that all people born into this world are children of God. Your first birth does not make you a child of God. In fact, there are some who are born and remain children of the devil. You are a born sinner. You must be born again to become a child of God. You must be Saved. You must accept Jesus as your Savior. You must live your life in a manner acceptable to God. You must do right and love that which is right. Only then will you be adopted into the family of God through your relationship with Jesus Christ. Those who are saved are children of God through faith in Jesus Christ. Your life must be led by the Holy Spirit. Only those who are led by the Holy Spirit of God are children of God. Only children of God will realize the inheritance offered to them by the Heavenly Father. Eternal life in God's paradise. No one said the road would be easy. Nothing this good can come without work, pain, sacrifice, discipline, and love.

Intentionally causing one's own death. Suicide. There are more reasons than can be here stated. They can all be summarized in the phrase hard times. The disability to coat with hard times. We can understand this traumatic stress more in children than in adults. Children are more subject to traumatic stress than adults. They need to be accepted and made to feel good about themselves. Suicide is the second leading cause of death among children. Even bullying can cause depression. With adults, the reasons for suicide can be physical, mental, or emotional. Over one million people each year take their lives simply because they see no way to change things. No hope for tomorrow. You can do a lot of research on the subject of suicide and you will never find the word hope. There is no life without hope. Regardless of how bad things are, hope must be alive if there is to be life.

Even on your death bed, you are hoping for a miracle. Your research will also never find the name of Jesus. The one factor that the vast majority of people who commit suicide have is that Jesus is not in their lives.

They do not understand that they can win their battle if they call on Jesus to help them. That is the reason God sent Jesus to us. To help us in times of need. The word made flesh. Jesus suffered hard times from birth to show us that we have no options. God is the only answer to our troubles and our lives.

Let me tell you something. This life ain't nothing to play with. If you are weak, it will kick your butt. If you think you can make it on your own, you are fooling yourself. Only the strong survives. Mama, daddy, wife, husband, child all will die. You will be standing there by yourself. Looking into space. Not knowing your right hand from your left. You don't have the courage to carry-on and you don 't know where to find it. You are so tired of this weak watered-down life. Why not commit sideways. It's a way out. Listen. Do you hear the footsteps behind you? Turn around. There are footprints behind you. Listen closely. My precious child, I never left you during your time of trial. It is I who will carry you. A great turn-a-round. Just because you have been beaten down does not mean that you will not have a great turn-a-round. Courage to keep on keepin on through the Spirit of God. You can see the vision of the promise leading into your destiny. You always had God's Spirit within you. Knowledge of God's love through Jesus. All the trials and tribulations of this world are weak before the Spirit of God.

We can last the storm because we know that we have the victory. The victory given to us by Jesus. The victory that lets us know of the love of God. That lets us know that regardless of what happens to us in this life, the best is yet to come. The victory that tells us what is truly important. That tells us that we are more than matter. That we have a heart inside of us that can never stop beating. A heart that no doctor can touch and a soul that can never die. Trouble will be all around us, but, it will never be in us. Pain, sorrow, grief will continue with us throughout this life, but, because of the Spirit of God nothing can stop us. Tears of joy. Hope for tomorrow even after death. Loving and trusting in our God. Believing that our future with Him will be wonderful.

Most people in this world do not know or believe in Jesus. There are numerous reasons. There are some people who live in countries where Christianity is a capital crime. A person could be killed for efforts to learn about Jesus Christ. Yes, the teachings and ways of the Pharisees and Sadducees are still present over two thousand years later. People of the free world have the opportunity to learn about Christ Jesus. Most do not take advantage of their opportunity. Some will not come out of the closet. We all are creators of habit. We even sit in the same seat when we go to church. People enjoy living in their comfort zone. They are not interested in learning anything new. They make excuses that help them justify staying in their comfort zones. They say, look at him. He is a Christian. If being a Christian will make me like him, forget it. There is only one reason that anyone who knows Jesus would not like Him. Self-promotion. It is to a person's earthly benefit to dislike Jesus. No non-self-centered person who has ever known Jesus has not liked Him. There are no just reasons for a person of the free world to not come to know Jesus. There are many people who have died to give us the opportunity to learn about Jesus. Peter, Paul, even Jesus Himself. They all died in an effort to reveal to us the love of God and the love of Jesus. It is for each of us to ensure that their deaths were not in vain.

The power of the Holy Spirit. As stated previously, possibly the greatest accomplishment of Jesus was to bring to us a source that will be with us forever. One of the most important functions of the Holy Spirit is to help us through this life. To help us make the correct decisions in life. Be honest with yourself. If you had the choice of living in this word forever or living in paradise with God, what would be your decision? Would you choose to never die? Would you rather live in this world forever than live in paradise with God? Well, You do not have the choice of living in this world forever. You will leave this life only to be the subject of Resurrection because you are a child of God. God is not a God of the dead but of the living. That is the reason He granted us the opportunity for ever-lasting life when we make the right decision. The most important decision you will ever make. Accepting God and Jesus into your life. For His children, making the correct decisions in this life is of primary importance to God. That is the primary reason He gave us the Holy Spirit. God will speak to you through the Holy Spirit each time an important decision has to be made in your life. His directions will lead you toward your destiny. Nothing in your life is more important than your destiny. Your purpose for living. Jesus told us this when He said the Holy Spirit shall teach you all things, and bring all things to your remembrance, whatsoever I have said unto you. When we accept God, Jesus, and the Hoy Spirit we have been saved and we will live forever.

# PROCLAMING THE WORD OF GOD

We remember people who gave their lives because to them letting the world know of their love for God and Jesus was more important than life. The bible is full of such people. People who would rather be killed than disclaim their God. People who were crucified. Who were stoned to death. Feed to lions. We cannot count the number of people who suffered and died believing in Jesus. You have read the bible. You know their stories. Yet, there are people today who go to church almost every Sunday who will not speak the name of Jesus outside of the walls of the church. Words are powerful. Some just want to be liked. Most people in this world do not believe in Jesus. Therefore, you will turn people off by talking to them about Christ Jesus. They say, oh here comes that holy one again. Who wants to hear all of that? Jesus said the world will hate you for My name sake because they do not know Him that sent Me. If being accepted and liked is more important to you than your relationship with God, it's time for some self-evaluation. Then there are those who inside don't think they are worthy to profess the goodness of God to others. They think, I know I am not all I should be. I feel guilty about some of the things I have done. So guilty that there would be a sense of shame if anyone knew about it. Me telling someone else about the goodness of God would be hypocrisy. I feel bad enough as it is. Becoming a hypocrite would only make it worse. It is true that you do not want to give a false impression. But, down inside of you, do you really believe that there is a lack of virtue or sincerity? You have sinned. You have also asked God to forgive you. You serve a loving caring God who has always been there to help you. You made a mistake, but, you are not a mistake. Now if I do that I would not, it is no more I that do it, but sin that dwelleth in me. You did wrong, but, God does not expect you to be perfect. It's time for you to accept the love, grace, and mercy of your Heavenly Father. You don't have to preach the gospel to let people know that you are a child of God. All you have to do is be yourself from the inside out. When you are speaking to people, feel relax and comfortable and let the Lord direct your speech as He directs your path. We can bring others to God by the way we live and the way we communicate. We can be effective agents of God proclaiming the word of the Lord.

# COVENANT

The word covenant is seldomly used in modern day English, however, the meaning is greatly a part of our everyday lives. We enter into agreements with regularity. Your automobile, residence, even your utilities are all financial agreements. Your marriage is an agreement to live your life with an effort to make another person happy till death do you part. You have entered into a covenant. A solemn promise or vow entered into with another human being. Yet, fifty percent of marriages end without death. That solemn promise was broken. When we are baptized and/or accept God, Jesus, and the Holy Ghost, we enter into a covenant with God. A solemn promise to live our lives in a manner acceptable to our Heavenly Father. Yet, too often we do not keep our end of the agreement. We commit acts which we know are not acceptable to God. There is one big difference in entering into a covenant with a human being and entering into a covenant with God. Forgiveness. Your spouse or creditor will hold you to your stated commitment. Forgiveness is not a part of the contract. Maybe it is not your fault. Situations change over which you have little control. Too bad. You will still be held accountable.

When we enter into a covenant with God, there is an understanding that the Divine One, knowing who He is in agreement with, will not demand perfection. No human being is or has ever been perfect. The lesson is that you have to know the person with whom you will enter agreement. You have to know that person's credit score. God knows more about you than you know about yourself. He knows what is in your heart. God is willing to give you a second and third chance to repent and try to do that which is right and just. He knows if you are truly trying. Accepting God into your life does not make you perfect. It takes time to grow in the Spirit of God. You are getting better each and every day. You are permitting God to order your steps. Direct your path. The covenant with God has a unique phrase written in it that you will not find in any other agreement. I will wait on you to become all that I want you to be because I truly love you.

The Old Testament tells us of a covenant with basic understanding being the laws of Moses. The Ten Commandments. Commandments that God knew imperfect human beings could not keep. God wanted us to understand our imperfection. He wanted us to realize our need for help. He wanted us to realize our need for a Savior. A perfect Savior. The only One who could wash away our imperfections before God. We now live under the new covenant of Grace. We do not have to be perfect to be acceptable to God. The life, suffering, death, and Resurrection of Jesus has washed away all of our sins past, present, and future. Our spirits are perfect before God because we will forever live under the covenant of the Grace of our Heavenly Father.

# THE BIBLE

In the Old Testament, we numerous times read the writings (God of Israel). This would make a person think that God was only the God of Israel. There had to be millions of other people and numerous other ethnic groups on the world at that time. Are we to believe that God only blessed the Hebrews and turned His back on all other human beings? Where are the writings of the other ethnic groups who lived during the times of the Old Testament? When we read the bible, we must understand that it was written entirely by Jews. It was written entirely by human beings. Human beings who meant well and believed deeply. Human beings, who because of human nature, put their own slant on their writings. They couldn't help it. They were human. They did not obey the command of God who ordered ye shall not add unto the word which I command you, neither shall ye diminish ought from it, that ye may keep the commandments of the Lord, your God which I command you. The Old Testament was written in Hebrew because it was written for Jewish ears. The New Testament was written in Greek because that was the dominate language of the Romans. Since then, the bible has been translated into numerous languages. We can reasonable state that the translators put their own slant on things that they could not understand. English is a new language compared to Hebrew. There are numerous Hebrew words for which there are no English words. Numerous times translator had to use, I think it means, in their translations. Or, did they write, I want it to mean? When rulers like Alexander VI, the ruler of Rome, took control they changed the bible to read as they wanted it to read. Thus, deceiving the entire world.

So, when we read the bible, what are we really reading? A document written by people who by human nature inserted their own slant. A document translated by people who by human nature inserted their own slant. A document that people by human evil nature made the writings of the bible as they wanted it to be. You only have to change or insert a few words here or there to make a false impression. There were plenty of people involved to do so.

Why should people love the bible? The bottom-line. Belief in God, Jesus, and the Holy Ghost. Yes, there are people all over the world who have never read the bible. Yes, there are languages into which the bible has never been translated, yet, people who understand only those languages believe. How could this be? The answer is the Holy Spirit. The Spirit of God has no limitations.

# DIVERSITY

God did not permit there to be different races of people for the purpose of separation. In reading between the lines, we see that the Jews separated themselves from all others. They translated the word of God in a manner that would accommodate their desires. Love thy neighbor as thy self. Jews considered only other Jews as their neighbors. Even when it came to inclusion, Jews believed that all others must adopt their traditions if they were to be saved. This is not the way of God. Jesus gave us the Great Commission. Go into ALL nations and spread the good news. Man has from the beginning of time interpreted God's word to suit his own purpose. Race has been a major deciding consideration.

There are so many differences in people because God wanted it that way. From the beginning, God desired diversity for the purpose of inclusion. There is no way that a black person could turn white or a white person could turn black. Adam and Eve were not white or black. They were brown. People who lived in hot areas of the world where the sun showed itself most of the year became dark of skin. People who lived in areas of the world where they realized less sun throughout the year became light of skin. This is not hard to understand if you want to understand it. How else could there be people of different colors?

There was a man name Josephus who lived during the time of Jesus. He reported the description of Jesus as black skin, short growth, eyebrows meeting, and an underdeveloped beard. Daniel was a servant of God given visions by God that no other human being could foresee. In one of Daniel's visions, he saw a man that all humans kind bowed down to. He described that man as having hair like wool. Read Daniel 7:9. This tells us that Jesus was a person of color.

The Moors were people of color. They worshipped the black Jesus. The Moors ruled Europe until the Roman Empire conquered them. The ruler of the Roman Empire at that time was Alexander VI. He had all pictures of Jesus destroyed and made the writings of the bible pure white. Again, an example of man changing the word of God for his own purposes.

Anyone who hates another because of the color of that person's skin has committed a sin before God. God wanted diversity among His people. God wanted inclusion among His people. God wanted love among His people. Hate is evil. You might think that you are not a hater. Then why do you stay in your comfort zone? Why are your friends all the same color? Why do you refuse to consider the view points of others? Your purpose for living should be to follow the word of God. Can you truly say that following the word of God is the purpose of your life?

# IS YOUR ALL ON THE ALTAR?

The silly games that people play. Every night and every day. Never meaning what they say and they don't say what they mean. Then they toy away the hours in their ivory towers. Till they are covered-up with flowers in the back of a black limousine. Oh, it's a good life to be free and explore the unknown. Till the heart-aches and you find you must face them alone. You are playing games with God without even knowing it. Are you a one day a week Christian? When you go to church, do you put a one-dollar bill in the offering when you can afford more. There are people who keep coming to you and asking for your help. You keep giving to them for all the wrong reasons. You really don't want to. You say to yourself, they never offer to do anything for me. All they want is to use me. We all would like to hear a thank you every now and then. We must ask ourselves, why has God placed me in a position to give instead of one who is asking for help? The answer is that you are favored. God has placed you in a position to help his people. He told you that the good you have done will be re-paid to you one hundred-fold. He did not say that your blessing would come from the source where you planted the seed. It didn't just happen. You have been blessed and placed in your present position to help other. Your blessing will come from God. We can do that which is right for the wrong reasons. Renewal of the mind. I am going to help you because God wants me to help you.

We must understand that a selfish person will never be successful. True success comes from above not from that which is earthly. We Christians must examine ourselves. Am I a selfish person? Am I giving to God only the left-overs financial, time, other people? That's what the devil wants. The devil wants you to keep giving as little as possible to God. Sometimes we wonder why this race is so hard to run. Why the test when we are doing our best? Maybe, it is because you are actually not giving your best. Why is God holding back my blessings? Want is God waiting on? God is waiting on you. God is waiting on you to lay your all on the altar. When you wake-up in the morning, why is it that you think about everything but God? Before you go to sleep at night, do you thank Jesus for guiding you safely through that day? When you walk pass that person who you don't care for, all you have to say is God loves you. That's all. You will immediately see a change in that person and in you. To become the unselfish person God wants you to be, you must step out of your comfort zones. We all must learn to give back to God unselfishly.

# EMPOWERING THE POOR

There are so many people who wake-up each morning knowing that they will not be any better off the next day than they are this day. They are living without hope. They can see no way to change things. No hope for tomorrow. There is no true life without hope. The problem can be any of a number of reasons. Health, finances, people. Most people who come into a lot of money only will use the money on themselves, those who are close to them, or they will waste it. Waste means without wisdom. Wisdom is the ability to distinguish between good and evil. Right and wrong. There are some things in life that seem and feel right, but are actually wrong. Most people lack wisdom. Most people lack faith. Their faith is based on circumstances. They do not have the wisdom to understand that which they have is a gift from God. It is not theirs to do with as they please. They are only overseers managers of that which belongs to God. They do not ask themselves, what would God have me to do with that which I have? Self-esteem is esteeming yourself. Having the wisdom to place yourself above circumstances. To place yourself above poverty, money, even the way things are now. Hope is looking forward not backward. Having faith that the best is yet to come. Believing that you have a heart inside of you that can never stop beating and a soul that will live forever. It's all in the mind. There is nothing in this world that you cannot live without with one exception. God. You have health problems, no money, no job, family problems, no roof over your head. You keep thinking that it can't get any worse. You have something that all of these circumstances cannot affect. The love of God. You only have to make Him your priority and follow His lead. All of those earthly distractions have been placed there by the devil. Money, family problems. All to distract your attention from your focus on God. You already have the victory given to you by Jesus. You have been empowered by the Lord.

# A MORE EXCELLENT WAY

There is faith, hope, and charity. The greatest of all is charity. Without hope there is no life. Faith opens up the possibilities for all things. How can anything be greater than faith in God? The greatest Commandment starts with the word love. The second greatest Commandment starts with the word love. God is telling us that above all He wants love to dominate our lives. He wants us to stop thinking about ourselves and think about charity to others. By following the second greatest Commandment, we are also following the first greatest Commandment. How can you hate one of God's children whom you have seen, yet, state that you love God whom you have never seen? There were people who hated Jesus because He was taking away their thunder. There are people who hate others because they do not look like they look. Is God color blind? The answer is NO. God knew exactly what He was doing when He made you white or black. Female or male. Love thy neighbor as thy self. The Jews, during the time Jesus was here on earth, considered only other Jews their neighbors. Do you consider only people of the same financial status your neighbor? Do you consider only people with the same belief as your neighbor? The same color of skin? The only factor that will get you into heaven is love. You can have all the faith and hope that any human being can have and it will mean nothing without love. Love is inclusive. Caring about God's people without limitation. You might dislike that which another person does. You might dislike the way another person acts. You might dislike the behavior of another. It goes deeper. When we see a person fail who has done wrong, we rejoice. We call that justice. It might be justice but it is not love. You should pray that the Holy Spirit will step into that person's life making a meaningful difference. That's love. Praying to God for the good and for the bad. Nothing can save this world. It is already lost. Most people are going to hades and there is nothing you can do about it. You can only help one person at a time through charity. LOVE. A more excellent way.

# THE CHOSEN FEW

The disciples were men of great faith. They were willing to give up their all to follow Jesus. However, they did not first choose Jesus. Jesus first chose them. You did not first choose Jesus. God first chose you. Before you were granted life in your mother's belly, God knew you. God had great plans for you. You had only to be born into this world and accept God as the Lord of your life. By doing so, you have been adopted into the family of God. God loved you before you were born. But, your birth into this world did not make you a child of God. Your first birth did make you a relative, but, it did not make you a relative of God. Upon accepting God as the Lord of your life, you were adopted. Being adopted is greater than all. No one is adopted by accident. God chose you to be His child. God ordained you to be fruitful. To do right and love that which is right. He gave you Jesus as your Savior. He ordained Jesus, who was without sin, to die for you a sinner. He gave you Jesus, who without limitations, to do that which you could not do. To help you do what you cannot do without Him. You are not God's servant. You are His heir. No one who has ever lived is more important to God than you. Not even Jesus. Not everyone can rightfully claim to be of the chosen few.

When God made the determination that you were the one He wanted as His child, He made an investment in you. He planted the seed of His spirit within you so that you would be fruitful. Your fruits must multiply. Your harvest must grow with each passing season. You must make a sincere effort to grow in the spirit of God. Giving your life to Jesus is more than talk. You must love that which is right. God's spirit is within you. The Holy Ghost will help you to make the right decisions in your life. The Holy Spirit is the reason you permitted God and Jesus into your life. God's spirit will continue to direct your path. Your path is greater than just waiting on the Lord. The more you know about God the closer you will draw to Him. We learn from two sources. One, divine intervention. The Holy Spirit will speak to you directly. Two, we learn from others. Our growth and inspiration will come from others. If you are the smartest person in the room, you are in the wrong room. *It is good to surround yourself with people you love and who love you. But, love is not enough. You must relate to people who can help you grow in God's spirit.*

*Jesus told us of the coming of false prophets. We must learn from others, however, we must depend upon the Holy Spirit to determine right from wrong. Humans are dangerous. Man has a history of changing God's word to read as he desires. God made the seventh day of the week the Sabbath Day. You will hear all kinds of reasons telling why you are going to church on Sunday the first day of the week. No human being had the authority to change a command of God.*

You will also hear numerous reasons why some Christian denominations consider sprinkling a form of baptism. Scripture clearly states the manner in which Jesus was baptized. Nowhere in scripture does it state that sprinkling is a holy substitute. The word fear is not a word that humans feel comfort with. Fear of the Lord. When you were a child, your parents would tell you that you would be punished for doing certain things. You did not do them because of fear of punishment. The human mind is designed to protect the body. As you grew older, you gained more understand. Fear of the Lord is the beginning of wisdom. We must accept God at His word and not change His word to accommodate our comfort level.

It is necessary for God's children to gain knowledge of God through sources other than the bible. By doing so, you will learn that Christ Jesus was a person of color. Yet, every picture you see will be a white Jesus. It is true that we do not care about the color of the skin of Jesus. But, no one likes to be lied to. The bible does not state the color of Jesus for a reason.

God's love has no limits. The children of God must understand the weakness of the human mind in learning about our Heavenly Father.

# I WANT TO GO TO HEAVEN

No one can prove that there is such a place. Atheist don't believe that there is a heaven. Therefore, nothing happens after death. The question has been asked, how were people saved before Christ? Some believe that they were not saved. People simply remained asleep until the birth and Resurrection of Jesus. Upon His Resurrection, they were the subject of His judgement and proceeded to heaven or hades. There are those who believe that human beings remain asleep and will remain asleep until the second coming of Christ. At which time, all will come out of the grave to face judgement. Everyone has evidence, yet, no one has proof. There are so many questions that will never be answered in this life. Scripture tells us what we want to hear. For most Christians, heaven is our goal our destiny. We might not like it, but, we know we will only be here a short period of time. Nothing is more important to us than going to heaven. Life has to have some meaning other than just here and now. We might even be afraid of death because we are not sure about that which happens after we leave this life. We have been told that our good deeds will have no determination. But, in the back of our minds we continue to believe that being a good person will help us to get to heaven. Surely God did not give us the Ten Commandments only to disregard our efforts to keep them come judgement day. Scripture tells us that we serve a just God who will not forget the good that we do for His children. Yet, God is not a score keeper. He will not add up our positives and negatives when passing judgement. We are also told that God knows our hearts. Those with a pure heart will see God. A pure heart is not easy to attain. Our hearts must be pure toward everyone not just the people we love. We must repent with a pure heart. There are many who believe that our sins are automatically forgiven because of Jesus. However, scripture tells us that if we do not repent, we will parish. This could only mean that we will receive forgiveness only if we seek it with a pure heart. Scripture also tells us that we will see Abraham, Isaac, Jacob all the prophets, in the Kingdom of God. This tells us that we will have a sense of recognition when we get to heaven. We will again see our earthly love ones.

We only have faith. God does not want us to have proof. Without faith, it is impossible to please God. There are some denominations that believe faith is not a factor in getting to heaven. They believe that only the Grace of God will make that determination. Yet, we believe that we must please God in this life in order to be saved. If faith has no determination as to being saved, what value is faith? For by grace are ye saved through faith. How many times in scripture have we read the statement your faith has made you whole? We believe in something we cannot see or touch. We believe we have a soul, yet, we cannot see or touch it. We believe in God whom *we cannot see or touch. Why do we believe without proof? Could it be that we are afraid not to believe? Is heaven that important to us?*

*This is the most important decision we will ever make in our lives. That is the reason it is so difficult. We will never figure it out. We can only come to God as would a small child trusting in His goodness. Faith reveals the presence of God in our lives. God wants us to surrender all. Lay our all on the alter. Give our lives to Him. All other factors will follow without effort. Good deeds and love without limitations.*

*Our efforts to get to heaven will make our lives better. Things don't seem to bother me like they use to. Encouragement, inspiration. The will to keep on keeping on through the Spirit of God. Salvation is free, but, it is not without cost. Freedom is free, but it is not without sacrifice. You want to go to heaven. It is going to cost you something. For many, the cost is too high. You have to take up the Cross of Jesus everyday of your life. Just going to church on Sunday morning will not get you to heaven. It takes a seven day a week commitment. You have to control the little things and the big things with a godly touch.*

*One of the greatest mistakes that a Christian can make is try to live life in a manner that pleases God. God gave us the Ten Commandments. It has also been stated that obeying some, but not all, of the Commandments will not please God. That is one reason you are a sinner. You are an imperfect human being trying to serve a perfect God. That will never happen perfectly. Therefore, you will always be a sinner. You will never be able to satisfy all the laws of Moses. With Jesus, we have a new Covenant. A Covenant that states like no other agreement you will ever know. A Covenant that reads, I will continue to love and protect you while you are growing in the Spirit of God. A Covenant that does not require you to be perfect. When we do good things, we should not do them to please God. We should do them because the Spirit of God is within us. When God looks at our hearts, He wants to find love. The reason we do anything is just as important as that which we do. People keep coming to you asking for money, loans, favors. You grant their request for all the wrong reasons. You think, all they want to do is use me. They never offer to do anything for me. We all want to be appreciated. But ask yourself, why is it that God has made me a giver instead of the one who is always seeking help? God has placed me in a position to help His children with a cheerful heart. I have been blessed. When God looks at your heart, He wants to see a pure heart. He wants to know that we serve Him out of love not out of what is in it for ourselves. The most important factor that will help get you to heaven is a pure heart. There are some evil people in this world. People who will do anything to anyone if they think they can getaway with it. God has told us that not all of them will fall in this life. But, they will fall. God will see to it. When they do fall before our eyes, we rejoice. We call that justice. It might be justice, but, it is not love. We should pray that the Holy Spirit will come into their lives and make a meaningful difference. That's love. Praying for the good and praying for the bad with a pure heart. Father, give me a pure heart so I may serve Thee.*

*Don't' worry about getting to heaven. Work hard to develop a pure heart. God and Jesus will take care of the rest.*

# TRUE TRUST

It's a test. A test to challenge your weakness. You cannot determine your level of trust without putting something on the block. Something that you value. Something that you do not want to lose. You might think that you have trust in certain people. People are funny. They never forget what you do to them, however, they find it difficult to remember what you have done for them. Trust in God is different. His pay back is different. With him or her, you are satisfied just getting back what you have given. With God, your return might not look like you expect it to look. God is primarily interested in your spiritual growth. He will return to you a hundred times more than you have invested. But there is a catch. The catch is designed to help you get to the next level. You can't get to the next level without help. The next level of spiritual growth. That person you loved who just passed away didn't first belong to you. That person belonged first to God. You are crying because you have lost a loving relationship. You are crying for yourself. You couldn't be crying for your friend because your friend is now in a better place than you are. If your friend left you a note stating that he or she loves you, and that he or she is going away to a place that will give them happiness forever. Deep inside, you would be filled with joy. We need to thank God for the children we still have. We need to thank God for the friends we still have. We need to trust God in good times and bad times. We need to thank God for loving relationships of the past and present. Nothing can happen to us that will keep us from trusting in God.

# LOVE

We wonder how haters get in controlling positions. We must come to the realization that this world is filled with haters. People who will walk into a church and commit mass murder. Think about it. There are black people alive today who have had relatives lynched during their life time. It has not been that long ago. They are still here. People who have committed these sins before God. They went to church on Sunday morning. Then went home got their lawn chairs and went to the park to see a black person lynched. I don't know about you, but, I have done some things in my life that I cannot even forgive myself for much less expect the forgiveness of God. Then I think about scripture. I think about Jacob who misused his brother and stole his birthright. God still loved Jacob. King David had a man killed so that he could steal his wife. God still loved David. Peter denied Jesus three times. Jesus still loved Peter. The first word of the Greatest Commandment is love. Love thy God. The first word of the second Greatest Commandment is love. Love thy neighbor. God is telling us that love exceeds all. Even faith. God wants our lives to be dominated by love. Love, no not just for one but for everyone.

# RENEWAL OF THE MIND

UNDERSTANDING. *Christians need to understand that doing right will not make you be right. That serving God does not mean that you go through life trying to please God. It is true that faith without actions is not true faith, but, actions without faith is dangerous. It will never be easy to understand. We might never be able to get it all straight. Maybe God wants it to be that way. Maybe He wants us to stop trying to figure Him out and just love and trust Him.*

*We wonder why in every church in America on Sunday morning we will find more women than men. When we think of the differences between women and men, the first think that comes to mind are the physical differences. Fifty percent of marriages end in court because couples do not understand that the differences between genders are deeper than physical. He won't even talk to me. Women are talkers. Women talk in circles. They don't keep problems building up inside of them as much as men. A man finds it difficult to discuss his personal problems with another person. He keeps his problems to himself. Each year over one million people take their own lives. 80% of them are males. These people simply cannot find a way to make things better and they do not want to continue to live in the center of the way things presently are. They want happiness, but, don't know how or where to find it. I don't suppose to be like this. What is going on with me? I'm trying to do all that I can, but, things never turn out right. I'm so sick of this weak watered-down life. God told us that man should not be alone. But, he needs someone who understands him. Someone who understands that there is a difference other than physical. Men also have a cycle in life. A recurring period within certain events of phenomena occur and complete themselves in a definite sequence. I am at this stage in life and look what I have accomplished. I don't see how it is going to get any better.*

*Maybe you are on the wrong highway. If you are in Ohio, you will never get to California headed east. Maybe you need a renewal of mind. You have been given the Grace of God. The grace of God is saving power. It can give you inspiration to be more than you have ever dreamed of. Grace is a gift that must be build upon. Too many of us do not use our gift because of a bad attitude. With the right attitude, it can take you to the next level. Understand, that you do not have to be concerned about doing right or living to please God. Give your heart to God. Love gives itself away. Start appreciating all the things around you that God has provided. Nothing can stop you now because you are a child of the Most High God. There has never been a person who has ever lived who God loves more than you. Renewal of your mind in the Spirit of God.*

# PREPARATION OF THE TABLE

Young children just sit down and eat. They do not think about the labor put forth to prepare the table. You are going through some things. The key word is through. It seems like if you are not coming out of a storm, you are going into one. Only the strong survive. The only way you can survive the storm is to be equipped. You must have on the armor of Jesus to keep evil forces from penetrating. If you have not prepared the table, you will not survive. You will weep what you sow. You wonder why it seems like it is always happening to you. God is preparing you. Fighting through the storm will make you stronger and wiser. You have to trust in the living God, who is the Saviour of all specially of those that believe. You must first prepare the table. God will provide the unleavened bread. Unleavened because as you grow in God's spirit, He will not change. God has planted a seed in you. You must water the seed and have confidence that it will produce good fruit. You have to wait and be patient. Often times, you must depend upon God for rain. There might be a drought. Hard times. However, you must believe in the power of God. If you do, you don't have to worry. God won't let you down. One day you will dance in the rain. God is developing you into a refined Christian. Hang in there. Bad times don't last always. The Lord is coming to save you. Nothing is too hard for the Lord. It will all happen because you have prepared the table. You are ready for the battle. Nothing can stop you now because you are a child of God. We must trust God during the good times and bad times. The bad times will tell what you are made of. You will survive the storm because the spirit of God is in you. When the spirit of God is in you, you will make that which you have left after the storm productive. You will live happily ever after because you were wise enough to prepare your table.

# WHY?

Why do you believe in something for which you have no proof? The answer to this question is very simple. You want to believe. You want there to be a God of love, grace, and mercy. You believe because you want to believe. Maybe you want to believe because you have been convinced. You have been brain washed. You have been told the story of Jesus since you were a child. You were taken to church before you knew what a church was all about. You were told to pray before meals and before going to bed. You saw your parents praying before you knew who they were praying to. You had no fear of God because you knew nothing about Him. You were told if you crossed the street without looking both ways, you would get your butt whip. You looked both ways because of fear not understanding. When you got older, you had more understanding and you still looked both ways. With understanding comes wisdom. When you grew-up, you realized that being an adult is only a trap. Without wisdom you would never get out of the trap. You didn't go through all of this when you were a kid. What happen and why did it happen? You now have the wisdom to understand that you are being crushed because God wants you to realize that you are nothing without Him. God wants you to have the mind-set to understand that you must seek Him first at all times. God wants to turn your need into feed. There can't be a miracle unless there is a need. Each time you reach back it is there. Jesus is always there to help you over the rough spots. You are now able to last the storm and march into your destiny because you know that God is ordering your steps and directing your path. You believe because deep in your mind and heart you know that there is a God who loves you. You only now have to fight a good fight. Stay the course. Keep the faith. The victory is yours.

# TRYING QUESTIONS

*Should I live my life trying to please God?*

We do things for all the wrong reasons. We give to others really thinking that they are only using us. They never offer to do anything for me. Yet, you continue to grant their request. Why? Is one of the reasons that you are trying to please God? Have you ever asked yourself, why am I a giver instead of the one who is always asking for a favor? God has placed you in the position and condition to help others. God has blessed you because He loves you. God wants us to love one another. Love one another as I have loved you. You will never have more than you need, however, you have found that there is always enough to carry-on. As long as you put God first, He will always be there when you reach back for more. Don't worry about pleasing God. Just give your heart and life to God. All else will follow.

*Was God only the God of Israel?*

Numerous times in reading the Old Testament we see the statement (the God of Israel). As if during those times, God was only the God of Israel. There had to be millions of other people and numerous other ethnic groups on the face of the earth during the times of the Old Testament. Are we to believe that God turned His back on all the rest of humanity and administered only to the Hebrews? Where are the writings of the other people who lived during those times? What were their stories?

*How were people saved before the birth of Jesus Christ?*

Some people believe that they were not saved. Others believe that they remained asleep until the Resurrection of the Christ. After which time they were taken before the judgement of Christ and their souls went to heaven or hades. Others believe that they are still asleep and will remain so until the second coming of Christ. There must be the understanding that the birth of Jesus into this world was not the start of the existence of Christ. Christ has always been at the right hand of God doing God's work. Jesus was with God before the creation of the world. Jesus created the world following the instructions of God. There were no people before Jesus the Christ. From the beginning of human kind, human beings have received salvation by faith in Almighty God and the judgement of Jesus Christ.

*Will God forget our good works?*

*We have been told over and over again that salvation comes only by the grace of God. That we cannot earn salvation. That our good works will have no weight come judgement day. You can't earn you way into heaven. Your good works come only because of your faith and love of God. We think, then God gave us the Ten Commandments for nothing. He does not care if we follow them or do not follow them. This just does not sound like the God I love. We serve a just God. Read Hebrews 6:10. God will not forget the kindness you have shown His people. God will not forget.*

*Will we have a sense of recognition when we get to heaven?*

*Only the pure in heart will see God. We want to see Jesus. We want to again see our earthly love ones. Luke 13:28 tells us that we will see the Prophets when we get to heaven. This is telling us that we will have a sense of recognition when we get to heaven. We will be again close to our earthly love ones.*

*Will only those who believe in Jesus Christ be save?*

*God has told us that He will have mercy on whom He will have mercy. God forgave Paul because of his unbelieve and ignorance. Jesus has stated that no one come to the Father but by Him. Is Jesus saying here that you must believe in Him to be saved? Or, is He simply saying that only He will make the determination as to who will go to heaven? Read 1 Timothy 4:10. God is savior of all especially those who believe. Especially those who believe. What does this tell you? Scripture tells us that there are some who will be least in the Kingdom of God. Will the statue of your belief have any degree of weight in your salvation? I don't know. However,, what I do know is that when you get to heaven the only person you should be surprised to see is yourself.*

# COMMUNICATION

You go through the routine. You read your bible. You go to church on Sunday. You are set in your ways. However, it seems that God is not paying an attention to you. Have you given Him notice that you want to grow in His spirit? God is going to pay attention to you only when you tell Him that you are hungry. He is not going to bless you because of your needs. He is going to bless you because of your appetite. You have to come out of your shell. You have to put some demands on yourself. It's cold outside. I'm going to bible study anyway. That person behaves in a disrespectful manner. The next time I see her, I'm going to say hello anyway. He is nothing but trouble. I'm going to pray for him anyway. You have to let God know that you are ready for an increase in blessings. You have to let Him know that you are hungry. Only then will He feed your appetite. It's the same old story of supply and demand. If there is no demand, there will be no supply. God hates waste. You must show Him that you are fruitful with that which He has already given you if you desire more. You think too much. You are going to think yourself to death. You worry too much. Worry is negative faith. Lack of faith in Jesus. Jesus has your back. Don't worry about what is behind you. Trust in Him. Hope is right behind you. Every time you reach back, there is a hand full of blessing there for you. There is a support entity that you can not even see but you know it is there. It gives you the mental and physical strength to keep on keeping on. Talk to God. When your ears hear it come out of your mouth, it does something to your heart. Let God know that you are ready for more of His blessings. He is waiting on you to tell Him. He will give you all that you want to satisfy your appetite. How hungry are you for the blessings of God?

# THE SPIRIT WITHIN

I feel comfortable in my presence with the Lord. What makes you think that God wants you to feel comfortable with Him? I went to church this morning. I said hallelujah three times. I even clapped my hands. I put a dollar in the offering. I know I am saved. You go to church on Sunday. What about the other six days of the week? Why do you expect more than you are willing to give? What do you want from your relationship with God? He has been good to you. You have a roof over your head, food to eat, clothes on your back. Is that all you want? That is all you are going to get if you do not wakeup. You think you are at peace with the world. As long as things go well around you, you are satisfied. It's a good life to be free. What happens to your peace when things are not so good? When there is no soft music in your ears. When storms keep blowing in your life. When you feel like if you are not coming out of a storm you are going into one. The peace of this world is not a sustaining peace. It changes with the conditions of your surroundings. When it stays bad for an extended period of time, in the midst of the storm, you could lose it all mentally and physically. God's peace is the answer. It's a fearful thing to fall into the hands of the Lord. To know that here is nothing that can keep you from trusting in God. That the storm can be all around you, but it will never be in you. That there is nothing that can happen on the face of the earth that will keep you from securing your purpose in life. The reason God created you. The spirit within. Inner peace. Life in this world is only temporary. I know that God has prepared a place for me where there is no pain or sorry. No crying and no tomorrow. Just every lasting peace and happiness in the presence of God.

# CONSCIENCE

Throughout the history of human kind there have been division. Jews and Gentiles, Protestants and Catholics, whites and blacks, Democrats and Republicans, democracy and communism, love and hate, good and bad. The list goes on and on. The most serious division could very well be the one talked about least. Those who believe in God and those who do not. Those who do not will do anything they think they can get away with. They kill, rob, steal, hurt other people at will. We ask ourselves why and how did they get that way. Human animals. Those who believe in God, believe they have an obligation to live their lives in a manner that is hopefully pleasing to God. They know they cannot be perfect. They know they are sinners. They know that there is a division between body and spirit. They know that they can never be perfect in body but they can be perfect in spirit because spirit comes from God and God is both perfect and spirit. Therefore, they must walk in the spirit. People who believe in God have been given something unique. Something that those who are without God do not have. A conscience. A gift from God that tells them that they have sinned and must repeat. Your conscience is never complimentary. It can only condemn. It can only let you know that you have done that which is not pleasing to God. God is love. God never condemns. Condemnation comes only from the conscience.

We must truly understand the sacrifice of Jesus. The meter is turned off because of His sacrifice. He has destroyed sin forever past, present, and future. There is nothing you can do about it. You are a sinner and you will always be a sinner. You are a sinner in body not in spirit. You are not that which you sometimes do. The devil is a liar and a divider. He wants to divide you from God. The devil can never divide you from the spirit of God because of the sacrifice of Christ Jesus. Your conscience lets you know when you have done wrong and must ask God to forgive you. It is a fearful thing to fall into the hands of the Lord. We come to understand that life is only a vapor that appears for a little time and then vanishes away. Our hope is in God alone. We have nothing else that we can depend upon. Nothing that will be with us forever. Only God.

# LOVE

Can anything be greater than faith in God? Without faith it is impossible to please God. Numerous times in the New Testament Jesus stated that your faith has made you whole. The greatest Commandment states Love thy God. The second greatest Commandment states Love thy neighbor. These two are God's greatest Commandments. Both start with the word love. Love is strong. It will make you do things you never dreamed of. King David had a person killed so that he could steal his wife. God loved David anyway. Peter denied Jesus three times, Jesus loved Peter anyway. Jesus said that He came to seek and save the lost. Because of love. Jesus underwent crucifixion because of love for His Heavenly Father and love for His Father's children. God so loved the world that He gave His only begotten Son. Love exceeds all. Nothing is stronger than spiritual Love.

We must grow in spiritual love for one another. Too often we find ourselves praying only for those we love. For those we care about. We turn our backs on those most in need of our prayers. The lost. Those who live their lives in a manner without regard to the will of God. When they fall before our eye, we rejoice. We call it justice. It might be justice but it is not love. We should pray that the Holy Spirit will come into their lives and make a meaningful positive difference. We should pray for the good and we should pray even harder for the bad. That's love. We can never grow in God's Spirit staying in our comfort zones. It might be hard but nothing is too hard for God. We must step out of our comfort zones and do that which is pleasing to God. We have to work to grow in the spirit of God. Nobody said the road would be easy. By doing His will you are showing your LOVE for your Heavenly Father.

# UNDERSTANDING WHAT IT MEANS TO BE SAVED

**T**HE TEN COMMANDMENTS - The laws of Moses were given to us to increase our understanding that we are imperfect people trying to serve a perfect God. It was stated that complying with some of the laws was not good enough. You must be true to all of the laws. Perfection is the only way this could happen. The only perfect person to ever walk this earth was Jesus. The Ten Commandments let us know that we need a Saviour because we will forever fall short of the glory of God. The Covenant of the Old Testament indicated that our salvation was dependent upon our performance as human beings. We have come to understand that our performance can never be perfect. The New Testament reveals that we do not have to be perfect to be saved by God because we have accepted the perfect Jesus as our Saviour. The life, death, and Resurrection of Jesus has perfected our Spirit before God. Our sins will not be a consideration in our judgment because of Jesus. We are saved because of what Jesus did for us not because of anything we do for Jesus. We now live under the grace of God not under the laws of Moses or this society. We will not be judged by that which we have done while on this earth. We will be judged by the reason we did it. Our spiritual hearts will determine our Salvation. God knows our hearts. Our actions are a reflection of our hearts. The pure in heart shall see God. We do not have to live our lives trying to please God. We do not have to worry about right or wrong. When we are born again, God controls our hearts. Our hearts control our actions.

Conscience – All human beings have one. When we are born again, God controls our conscience. We will sometimes sin, however, our conscience will let us know that we have done wrong. That we must seek the forgiveness of God and turn from our sinful ways. The key words here are born again. Some who have not been born again, have a conscience that has been damaged to the extend that it does not reflex evil. Our conscience is truly a blessing to those who believe in God.

We must understand that this is earth not heaven. We must understand that being saved does not mean that there will be all good and no bad. There are good angles and bad angles. There are good spirits and bad spirits. There are good people and predators. Good animals and those whom care only about themselves. When we are saved, we care about God and His children. When we are saved, our hearts our filled with God's love. We are no longer afraid of death. Death only brings us closer to God.

We believed we have been saved because we have accepted Jesus Christ as our Lord and Savior. We worry about others whom we love. Who live a Godly life but the name God and

Jesus never comes out of their mouths. We wonder if they will make it to heaven. Jesus said that no one comes to the Father but by Him. Many believe that this statement means we must believe in Jesus to be saved. Others believe that Jesus is only stating that He alone will decide who will be saved. The Apostle Paul stated that he had been forgiven because of his ignorance and unbelief. It is possible that God will forgive others as He forgave Paul. God has told us that He will have mercy on whom He will have mercy.

It is a good feeling to believed you have been saved. To believe that you will experience everlasting life in the house of God Almighty. You got shoes. I got shoes. All God's children got shoes. When I get to heaven going to put on my shoes and walk all over God's heaven.

We seem to think that everyone will be equal in heaven. Jesus has told us that some will be considered the least of these in heaven. He is telling us that all will not be equal in heaven. Jesus also told us that He will return not in consideration of sin but to bring salvation to God's children. That He will give each exactly what is deserved.

He could not mean in this life. He could only mean in heaven. If you deserve more. If you have given more to God in your earthly life, you will receive more in heaven. Everyone who is saved will not be of equal status when they get to heaven. You will receive exactly what you deserve. Those who have put forth more effort to live their lives to the will of God will receive more of God's glory in heaven.

We often wonder about perfection. It is easy to sin. It is difficult not to sin. Sin is sweet to the mouth but bitter to the stomach. You don't have to do anything to sin. Just sit there and breathe in God's free air. Don't lift a finger to help anyone. Just be a I ain't no trouble Christian and you have sinned. If you are truly saved, you will live like you are saved. You can never be perfect in the fresh the body. You can be perfect in the Spirit. God is Spirit. Once you have been born again you have been saved. You are not that which you sometimes do in the flesh. Your weakness has been washed away by Jesus. All things are new. You can never have a negative effect on your Spiritual being. Your soul has been anchored in the Lord. You will forever be spiritually perfect before God.

# ONE SIDE OF SIN

We are not sinners because we sin. We sin because we are sinner. Sin is a part of our nature. It's easy to sin. It is difficult not to sin. You don't have to take a lesson in lying. You don't even have to practice. You are a natural liar. It is part of your nature. When we think of sin, we think about things that we have done that we should not have done. Some people think, I know I'm going to heaven. I know I have been saved because I have never done anything to anyone. There is another way to sin other than stated in the Ten Commandments. Not doing that which you had the opportunity to do. Not doing that which you were given the physical and mental capacity by God to do. You don't have to do anything to sin. Just sit there and breathe in God's free air. Don't lift a finger to help anyone. Just be a I ain't no trouble Christian and you have sinned. As much as ye did it not to the least of these, ye did it not to me. You have to use what God blessed you with to glorify God. God foreknew you. God predestined you. God called you. He will glorify you if you glorify Him.

Justification is a word we must dig deep to understand. We have been told that we can not earn our Salvation. That our actions here on earth will have no weight come judgment day. Only the Grace of God will determine our Salvation. Then we remember the Ten Commandments. We wonder why God gave us the Ten Commandments if He cares not our efforts to live by them. One person dedicates years of his/her life to living with and caring for the sick, poor, and needy. Another person walks into a church with a gun and kills a dozen people. Are we to believe that the actions of the murderer will not be remembered come judgment? Are we to believe that the life of giving of the person who for years helped others will not be remembered by God? We are told that because of Jesus all sins past, present, and future, have been washed away. Our sins will not even be a matter of consideration before God.

Justification is a word we must dig deep to understand. How could Jesus tell the thief who was beside Him when on the Cross, this day you will be with Me in paradise? A thief. A person who has seriously hurt others. The answer is (it is not what we do but our reason for doing it) that will be in judgment. God has told us that our ways are not His ways. God knows our hearts. We have two hearts. One that pumps blood through our veins to our organs. One that is our Spiritual Heart. The person who walked into a church and murdered twelve people had a spiritual heart filled with the hate and sickness of the devil. The person who for years helped the sick, poor, and needy had a spiritual heart filled with the love of God. Jesus has provided justification before God for our actions. Jesus suffered greatly to do so. He was beaten nearly beyond recognition. No movie or book you will ever see or read will tell His degree of suffering. Jesus accepted this treatment because of His love for God and His love for God's children. His love for you before you were even born. Don't try to understand it. We will never be able to understand. When Jesus suffered, God suffered for you. Justification. We have been Glorified by God.

# ONLY THE GRACE OF GOD

We have been told that our salvation will only come from the grace of God. That we cannot earn salvation. That which we do in this life will not play a part in our judgment. This is not a race. Not, I am going to do more good than you so that my soul will shine brighter in the eyes of God. Your judgment will be based upon the reasons you do that which you do. Your judgment will be based upon your spiritual heart not your actions. There are rewards for your good deeds while here on earth. Mark 10:29 tells us that we will be blessed 100 times more than our gifts to others in this life. When we read that our earthly deeds will have no effect upon our salvation, we begin to think that our earthly good deeds are meaningless. This is not the case. We are told in Matt 16:27 that Jesus will return to bring salvation to those who wait. We are told that He will give to each exactly what is deserved. Upon the return of Jesus, the earth will be destroyed. This could only mean that we will receive what we deserve in heaven. Rev 20:12-13 tells us that we will be judged according to our works. Our works here on earth. These writings tell us that the good we do here on earth will be recognized and rewarded by God. When we get to heaven, we will receive exactly that which we deserve. There will be no equality in heaven. Jesus has told us that some will be considered the least of these. Some will live in a mansion. Some of us will be lucky to get an efficiency apartment. The degree of God's glory that you will receive will be determined by your degree of obedience here on earth after you have been saved. Those who have made any effort to live in the light of God will receive more of God's glory when in heaven. Those who have placed their earthly desires before the will of God will receive less of God's glory. The good that you do is recorded in the Book of Life which is kept by Jesus. If your name does not appear in this Book, you will not be glorified by God. You will not be saved. Your name will only appear in the Book of Life if you have lived a life satisfying in the sight of God.

We serve a loving God. Full of grace and mercy. God has been merciful to mankind since the beginning of civilization. God did not bring His judgment upon Adam and Eve for disobeying Him. He put them out of the garden because He did not want them to live forever in sin. Cain killed his brother Able. God did not bring His judgment upon Cain. He knew that Cain was a born sinner. God protected Cain to keep others from killing him. Not even Abraham was perfect. His wife was his half-sister. Jacob was a sinner. He took two sisters as his wives. Yet, God's grace and mercy followed them all of their lives. Only when man began to abuse the goodness of God, did He place the laws of Moses into effect. Humans started to believe they could get away with anything without realizing the wrath of God. God had been too good and too merciful. He had to bring a sense of order to humanity. Fear was all humanity could understand. The Ten Commandments were given to us to make us realize our imperfections. We would have to be perfect to satisfy all stated in the Ten Commandments. This could never happen, therefore, man needed the help of a Savior. A perfect Saviour. God's plan to send Jesus into this world was present when He gave us the Ten Commandments. God knew that we could never defeat sin without a Savior. Sin could only be defeated by Jesus. Through Jesus, the Grace of God will be with us forever.

# PERFORMANCE BASED FAITH

Why do you go to church? The first answer that will come out of your mouth is to praise the Lord. Your second answer, rather you will state it or not, is that you are thinking about yourself. You want to please God because deep inside you cannot keep from thinking that your behavior will help win God's acceptance of you. You are living under a false belief. You cannot stop thinking that your performance during this life will play a part in your salvation. God does not care if you are holy or not. We need to ask ourselves some questions. Why am I singing in the choir? Why do I usher every week? Why do I put money in the offering plate? If your reason is to help increase God's favor with you, you are living a pipe dream. If you are to be permitted a place in God's paradise, it will be because of that which Jesus did for you not what you do for Jesus. God wants to know that you have faith in Him. No, not surface faith but inner faith. God knows you are a sinner. He knows that you will never be worthy of His blessings and kindness. He Knew Abraham was a sinner. Abraham took his half-sister as his wife. Yet, God made Abraham the father of all nations. The point is that God is not going to pass judgment on your earthly performance. That will only come if you make it to heaven. God will pass judgment on your heart. The reason you did that which you have done. Is your heart filled with earthly desires or the will of God? What is the true degree of faith you have in God? When things are hard and seemingly out of control, do you worry or do you have faith that regardless of the outcome you will never stop loving and trusting in God? Faith is the difference between where you are now and where you want to be. It is true faith without works is dead. But, works without faith will kill you. You cannot get to where you want to be in life without faith. True faith means we believe that God will never give up on us. There is a difference between unbelief and a lack of belief. Between healing and being made whole. The degree of your faith and belief will be measured during hard times. Just because God has forgiven you does not mean that you have been saved. Just because you have been healed does not mean that you have been made whole. You can determine your degree of faith by looking into your heart. Your heart will control your mind and your mind will control your actions. You don't have to worry about doing right or wrong when you have been saved. When you have been born-again, your heart is controlled by God. Your mind and actions will reflex the goodness of God. You don't have to do anything but give your life to Jesus. God will take care of the rest. Your second reason for going to church might be self-interest. That's ok if your interest is growing in the spirit of God.

How good it feels to believe that you are under the umbrella of God Almighty. We should praise God for who He is. The wonderful things He has done in our lives. This includes not only the physical things He has done but more important turning us into people who desire to live life from the inside out.

# YOUR ALL ON THE ALTER

It is true that most people in this world do not believe in Jesus. It is true that on Sunday morning more people drive pass your church than are on the inside. Most people will never be saved. The most that the Christian faith can hope for is to bring one soul at a time to God. Christianity will always be in the minority when we consider the rest of this world. There is nothing that can be done about it. There are certain things in life over which we have no control. Black people will forever be in the minority in the United States. Lions will forever kill other animals for food to eat. That is their nature. People will forever be sinners. That is their nature. It is very difficult to change nature. All Christians can do is fight a good fight, stay the course, and keep the faith. Fighting a good fight is more than that which it might appear to be. Yes, there are more people driving pass your church on Sunday morning than inside. However, the problem is greater than that. All the people inside the church are not really inside. Just because you place a chair in a garage and make that your seat does not make you a car. Just because you come to church does not make you a true Christian. You see, everyone who attends church services do not attend to serve. A casual Christian is a person who is shadow boxing with God. A person who does not want God to change his/her life. Just be there in times of trouble. Help out when needed. A person who just wants a little bit of Jesus. All they want to do is add Jesus to their present agenda. God seldomly comes to mind Monday through Saturday. A Sunday morning Christian. Casual Christians are a major concern of Christianity because there are really no answers to the problem. Casual Christians have heard it all. They know as much about scripture as anyone else. Yet, it has not made for a change in their lives. Believe it or not, we can detect a change in our lives more Monday through Saturday than on Sunday. Thinking about being a person who wants to follow Jesus every day. Not just on Sunday. To follow Jesus requires a great deal of effort. You have to want to change. You have to believe that change will make for a better life. You have to dig deep to learn and understand the blessings that God has for you. You cannot be afraid to leave the shallow waters and venture out into deeper waters where you will find the blessings for your destiny. A Christian can continue to go to church on Sunday with fine clothes on and look acceptable to others but will never be acceptable to God. The Holy Spirit has to take control of your heart, mind, and actions. You have to want to grow closer to God. You have to make the decision that nothing in life is more important to you than being close to God. There is absolutely nothing that can be done to change a causal Christian other than prayer. Pray that the Holy Spirit will find a home in their hearts. Ask yourself, is my all on the alter seven days a week? Are you all the way in? Is the Lord deep down in your heart? Or, do you wake-up Monday morning feeling different from what you felt Sunday morning. You see, it should not be the church. If your primary relationship with Jesus is through the church, you do not have a personal relationship with God. The only reason you put on your best clothes to come to church is because you want to look and be your best when you walk into God's house. It makes you feel good. But really God is not interested in what you look like. God is interested in who you are inside. Your heart is your driving force. Everyday of the week you must want God to control your heart. You must live the life you sing about in your song. Oh, I feel so sorry for people who have never experienced this feeling in their lives. I can't describe this feeling. It is beyond words. All I know is that I am so glad the Lord came into my life.

# PROVE IT

In a court of law, it must be proven beyond a shadow of a doubt. Billions of people believe in God without any proof what-so-ever. The fact is that those who do not believe in God also have no proof. Religion is based on belief and faith not proof. Regardless of what you believe, no one can prove you wrong. The vast majority of people in this world do not believe in Jesus. Christians cannot prove them wrong. Some believe that their salvation will prove them wrong. Because you believe does not make you right. There are many whose souls are in a state of poverty. There are those who believe without even knowing it. Belief by it self is meaningless. Faith is more than words. There is an understanding that must come to all who believe in God. The understanding that we are not meant to understand God. Man has been trying to figure out God from the beginning of time. If God is so full of love, why is there so much destruction, pain, and suffering in this world? We must understand that we were not meant to understand. *I am that I am means that no one will ever understand God. We must also understand that we will only have one chance to get it right without cost. Grace without cost is a one-time blessing. When you drop the ball the first time. When you show a lack of appreciation for God's initial act of grace, you will have to pay the cost for a second chance. Because you have been forgiven does not mean that you will not have to pay for your mistake. The second time around, you will have to prove to God that you will be most appreciative. You will have to get up off of your knees. Prayer will not overcome laziness. God is not going to give you anything other than an opportunity. Remember the land of milk and honey. The Promised Land. It belonged to someone else. If you were not willing to fight for it, you would never have it. You have to prove to God that you want and appreciate His blessings. The doors that He has opened for you. The opportunity He has granted you. You can do this by an expression of faith. Showing Him that your roots are in the Lord. That your soul has been anchored in the Lord. Until faith comes home, it does not matter where it travels. You know that faith has come home when you can stand strong through the storm and rain in your life. It is the hard times that make you strong. Jesus picked Judas because He knew that the bad would be more of an assist to His purpose than the good. Fighting through the wars in your life will make you realize the strength of God. Will make you realize that nothing, life or death, can exceed the glory of Almighty God.*

# YOU AIN'T ALL THAT

You have a good heart. You have tried to help other people when possible. You have gone out of your way to help others numerous times. You have worked long and hard to support your family. You have been available whenever needed by your friends. You have donated numerous hours to your church. Yes, you have done some wrong things, but, nothing so bad that it would even began to have more weight than the good you have done. You often wonder why numerous people along the way have acted like they would prefer that you disappear. You have done nothing to them. In fact, with many you have been an assist to their lives. There are a very few who understand who you really are. A few who respect who you are. You sometimes get tired of being used. People who you have given to all of their lives seem to take you for granted. You are so tired of giving and really getting nothing in return. You know that the reason you give is not for personal gain. However, we are all human. Maybe you are looking at the whole picture wrong. Maybe you are looking for positive returns from the wrong sources. Your return might not come from those to whom you give. Scripture tells us that we will be blessed one hundred times more than our gifts to others. One hundred time more in this life. Your blessings will come from angels sent your way by the One who controls all. Stop burning yourself out trying to be all to everyone who says they need you. You are not a machine. You have to take a break in life sometimes and smell the roses. Refresh. Get your strength back mentally and physically. Stop being so concerned about other people. Believe it or not, they will find a way without you. You ain't all that. Spend some time with your Creator. Your life is important too. Maybe it's time for you to start paying some respect for and to your life. God put you here for two purposes. Yourself and others. You show God appreciation by paying respect for both. Love thy neighbor as thy self.

# OVERCOMING LIFE

Problems after problems. If we are not coming out of a storm, we are going into one. It seems that at best all you can do is keep up. Getting ahead is nothing more than a dream. While keeping up, it seems that you are just waiting for something bad to happen. That is all life is, keeping up and fighting through the bad times. You hear of people who have it worse than you. People who do not even have clean water to drink. Earthquakes, tornadoes, hurricanes, fires, water washing away people's lives. People hurting other people. People with all kinds of critical health problems. This world has always been that way. It is not going to change. You know that there is nothing you can do about it. What is the point of it all? Just keep living the best you can until you die. People who you love will die. They will only be with you a short period of time. Life itself is only here for a short period of time. You really don't know what to expect after this life. You know what you believe and you hear what other people tell you, however, you really do not know. It was obviously meant to be that way. No control of the present and no knowledge of the future. You came into this world with nothing and you will leave with nothing. It's difficult. It seems meaningless until you think about God. You realize that this world is not your permanent home. It is difficult but you will only have to put up with it for a short period of time. God created you. God has prepared a place for you where all of these problems and concerns will not exist. It's wonderful. At last, you can be at peace while living this life. Peace is not the absence of trouble. It is the present of the Lord in your life. Because of God and your belief in the future He has for you, you know that you will be safe at home. Safe in the care of Almighty God. Because of the love of God, you can in the name of Jesus of Nazareth rise up and walk.

# OUR SINFUL NATURE

Momentary satisfaction verses eternal blessings. Human beings have a sinful nature. It is not easy to change nature. The only thing that stops many from doing certain things is penalty. Some will do anything they think they can get-a-way with. Human Kind has a very wide nature. There are those who would never keep anything that does not belong to them. They would go out of the way to find the owner. Then there are those who would consider the same circumstance an opportunity for self-enrichment. Momentary satisfaction has destroyed many people. Not all momentary satisfaction is negative. We go to amusement parks for that purpose. Like most things in life, momentary satisfaction is only of benefit if there are no negative after effects. People who can control their behavior are wiser and more mature. I like to eat, however, I know that overdoing it will cause a health problem. I like sweets. But I know that because of diabetes I better control my desire. There are ways and means to help people control their sinful nature. A strong belief in God is one way. Growing in God's spirit helps to build character that can defeat sinful momentary satisfaction. It is true that Jesus suffered and died to wash-a-way our sins past, present, and future. However, His sacrifice removed the penalty of sin only. The practice of sin still remains. The practice of sin is that which we must work through. If you stay around bad people long enough, you will start to adopt their ways. Whatever you yield to the most you will become. When you yield to that which is good that which helps you grow in God's spirit, you understand that there are some things in life that are beneath you. You are better than that. The fire cannot come where it has already been. Jesus died to give you the chance to successfully work through these negative moments of momentary satisfaction. Your character has developed to the point of no return. You feel good about yourself. Your sinful nature is under your control. Praise God.

# WHAT'S IN IT FOR ME?

You love the Lord. You also love yourself. Why are you so full of religion? What if there was nothing in it for you? What if you knew that there were no earthly blessings? What if you believed that death was the end of it all? How strong would be your faith? Why do you praise God? Your answer might be for who He is. Would your answer include His blessings to you? You are a human being. That said, you cannot stop thinking about yourself. Yes, you pray that God will continue to bless you and yours. Yes, you pray for good health and a good life. You spend more time praying for yourself and yours than you do praising God. Do you love yourself more than you love God? Why do you want there to be an Almighty God and a after life in paradise? Is the reason, that you what to live forever even after you leave this life? You really do not understand God. You really do not understand why so many people die from floods, fires, tornadoes, hurricanes, earthquakes. You believe that God controls all. Even if he did not make it happen, He can keep it from happening if it is His will. If there was nothing in it for you, you would find it somewhat difficult to give God the praise simply because of your lack of understanding. When you think of all that you have read above, you feel somewhat uncomfortable because you know it is true yet you can do nothing to change it. The secret is, God wants it that way. God wants you to love yourself. God wants you to love yourself so much that you love Him for loving you. That's human nature. You love people here on earth primarily because they love you. You should not feel bad about the fact that your love for God is there because of your love for self. Yes, we all should love God because of who He is. We should love God with all our heart, mind, and strength. When God tells us to love thy neighbor as thy self, He is telling us love of self is a command. You cannot love your neighbor until you love yourself. The greatest gift God has given you is life. You show Him appreciation by taking good care of yourself inside and outside body and soul. Taking care of yourself is more than the obvious. You have to reach for what you truly want. Seek and thee shall find. When opportunity knocks, you have to jump at it. When God tells you to do something, do it. Don't think about it. God has already examined all of the possibilities. He is an all-knowing God. All you have to do is follow His lead. All you have to do is give to God the most precious gift He has ever given you. YOUR LIFE.

# CHURCH

You have been going to church as long as your can remember. It is now a part of your life. You have heard a thousand sermons. You are not likely to hear anything that you have not heard before. You have read the bible. The truth is, you really have never taken time to dig deep and try to understand that which you have read. But, is it really necessary? Will your love of God and Jesus be enhanced by your deeper understanding? When you leave church, you should not be the same as when you entered. You should feel closer to God. It makes you feel better just being in the house of God. Church is somewhat a social affair. You have many friends at church. People who you really care about. People who believe as you believe. People who you like being around. Church is really a support group. If your primary connection with Jesus is through the church, you do not have a sincere relationship with God. Most people go to church once a week. What about the other six days? Are you a Sunday morning Christian? What part does God play in your life Monday through Saturday? Do you consult God before making important decisions in your life or only when you need help getting out of bad decisions? Believe it or not, there are people in this world who permit God a larger part of their lives than you and they never go to church. Some don't even have a church to go to. Then there are those who go to church almost every week with their fine clothes on. They look acceptable to others but will never be acceptable to God. God does not care what you look like. God cares about who and what you are inside. Not only when other people are looking like in church. When God is inside you, you don't care what other people think. People can talk about you all they want and it will not mean anything to you because you know yourself. You know God and God knows you. You have a seven day-a-week relationship that no human being can penetrate. They can put you in solitary confinement. They can take every physical thing you have away but they can never take your God away. Church is good. You go to church to join together with others to praise God. But you know something. God inside is better. God inside is everything.

# IT'S A TEST

This is earth not heaven. Yes, it was meant to be heaven on earth but Adam and Eve messed that up. Sin has been a major part of humanity ever since. Not all bad things happen because of sin. Some bad things happen because God wants to draw us closer to Him. It is true that hard times draw us closer to God. Some hard times happen to us because of the power and blessings of God. Why? Why am I in this wheel chair while others are walking around with good legs? Why do I have cancer? I have tried to live right and do the right things. Why is this happening to me? Why did God take my child? Why was I born like this? Why, why, why? First, we must understand that God loves us. Secondly, we must understand that our reason for being here is to grow closer to God. God never puts you through anything without purpose. God wants you to learn from your negative experiences. Use your negative experiences to grow closer to Him. Growing in the spirit of God is our most important demand. There are people all over this world who are suffering. People born into poverty. People who do not even have enough food to eat or clean water to drink. People born physically mal-formed. This is earth not heaven. We will never be without pain and suffering. Only when we realize that our presents on earth was never meant and will never be of major importance, will we live life in peace. We will laugh and we will cry. We will feel good and we will hurt. It is a test. Through it all, will you continue to love and trust in God? Will your life experiences draw you closer to God? Nothing else in life matters but being close to God. Your birth was a blessing of God and your death will be a blessing of God. That's all that counts. GOD.

# EXTREME

How many times have you heard people say it's God's will? How many times have you heard people say God controls all? There are some things in life that we are not to understand. We do not understand how a little seed turns into an apple tree. There are some things in life that we simply must accept without full understanding. There is grace and there is faith. Grace is God's part. Faith is our part. We serve a loving God. God does not place bad things in our lives. He is not the cause of your health problems. God never does anything without reason. Without love. God put you here on earth to grow in His spirit. Everything He does is with that in mind. Growing in His spirit means that your faith in Him will continue to increase. He has made grace available to us. We must activate His grace by our faith. Faith that regardless of what happens in this life, we will never stop loving and trusting in God. We like to believe that God controls all. God does not control all. He has the power to control all, however, He controls only that which serves His purpose. There are some people who believe that it does not matter what they do. God is in control. Regardless of what they do in life, nothing will change because God has already made His decisions. It's His will. These are people who are living in the extreme. They believe that increased faith in God is meaningless. We must understand that God does play an active part in our lives. He is responsive to our trials and tribulations. That is what we mean when we state that we serve a living God. We can activate His grace in our lives by our faith. Believing that He is with us each and every day. Having faith that He will walk and talk with us when we let Him into our lives. There are somethings we will never understand. Why so many people die from natural disasters. But that is part of the test. Faith in God without understanding. We walk by faith not by sight. We were not meant to figure out God. We were placed here to love and have faith in Him. Not extreme faith to the point of belief that nothing we do matters. Faith that how we live our lives is meaningful to God. God does not do anything without reason. Do you really think that God gave you life without reason? Thinking that nothing you do in life will have an effect upon God is a lack of faith. God gave you life and He told you how to live it. The degree of your belief and faith in Him will be stated by the way you live your life.

# IT IS WHAT IT IS

We might never know the true word of God. The nature of man is the reason. Man is not to be trusted. Scripture has passed through more human hands than we can count. Man has infected God's word with an attempt to promote his own believes. It happened early in history and it is still happening today. God made the Sabbath Day the seventh day of the week. Man changed it to the first day of the week. The color of the skin of Jesus Christ is not stated in Scripture. Why is it that every picture you see of Christ Jesus is white? Could it be that man wanted Jesus to look like himself? In Scripture, Jesus stated while on the Cross, God why have you forsaken Me. Jesus is the Son of God. He was with God before coming to earth. Do you really believe that Jesus lost faith in His Father? Man wrote Scripture. Man had the opportunity to insert any wording that pleased him. Do you actually believe that God supported slavery? In reading the Old Testament it is obvious that human beings inserted their own feelings, believes, and customs into Scripture. It is what it is. You cannot change the Word to fit the person. To fit your own reasoning. We Christians must understanding what we are reading. We must understand the history of the bible. We must understand the nature of human beings. We must be able to look pass that which we have been told and feel that which God has placed in us. Feel God and Jesus working each day in our hearts and minds. The complete correctness of the bible does not matter. God and Jesus, that is all that matters.

We must also come to realization concerning life. You see signs stating that life is good. Was life meant to be good? Was life good for Jesus? Humans were meant to suffer. Our bodies were made to hurt and die. You wake-up in the morning and try to be happy. You have to go to work to pay bills even if you do not want to. You try to make the best of your situation. You try to find moments of happiness were ever you can. I cannot remember one Scripture in which Jesus was having a good time. There are seven billion people in this world. There will come a time in your life in which you will go through the whole day and never say one word to anyone. You were born to have a lasting relationship with God and God alone. It is what it is. This life is what it is. We were not placed here to have a good time. We were placed here to find peace, joy, and contentment through our Lord. Accept life for what it is. Laugh when you can. But understand that your joy is not of this world. God is the center of your joy.

# LOST FAITH

It is so easy to lose faith in God. There are so many negatives that will blind us to the love of God. Where is my God? I have been told that I have a life threatening disease. I don't have a job and can't find one. A love one just died. A tornado blew my home away. I am getting old. There are so many things I still want to do for people and for the Lord. I will never have the financial resources so I just waste away the hours waiting on death. Where is my God? I have been told that God controls all. Nothing can happen without His permission. Why is God doing this to me? We ask ourselves why God continues to permit the devil to exist. We believe God could destroy Satan with one word. God has a goal and a purpose. God does not control everything. He has the power to control everything, however, God controls only that which is a benefit to His purpose and goal. Our parents made a serious mistake when we were born. They lead us to believe that the purpose of life was happiness. They never had a conversation with us to inform us that life was designed to be painful. That we will fight mental, emotional, and physical pain, evil, and suffering all of our lives. We will find a million reasons to lose faith in God. God is very selective as to who He permits into His kingdom. He will permit you to go through hadesl to find out if you belong. Only when you reach the point of believing that nothing in this life can keep you from loving and trusting in God, will you be acceptable in His sight. Satan has many ways to tempt you. To get you to turn your back on God. The devil is a liar. Nothing he does should have an effect upon your relationship with your Heavenly Father. The devil's primary weapon is fear. Fear that the worse is coming your way. Satan wants you to love yourself so much that your love for God is secondary. Don't let Satan make a fool of you. Don't let the devil lock you out of heaven. Don't let him take away your blessings your Salvation. Tell the devil to go to hades or some other hot place. You came into this world with one thing and you will leave with one thing. The love of God. That's all you really need. The love of God.

# ATONEMENT

When Jesus died, mankind immediately had access to our Heavenly Father. Our sins would no longer separate us from our Creator. There was a curtain in the Temple that was so large it took 300 priests to separate it enough for the High Priest to go behind only on the Day of Atonement. The veil was 60 feet long and 30 feet wide. The purpose of the veil was to appease the sins of mankind of the wrath of God. The veil separated man from God. The place behind the curtain was the Holy Place. Jesus said that no man could take His life. That He gave it freely. Jesus gave His life to give mankind direct access to God. Twenty-four seven access. 365 day a year. Do longer would there be anything standing between God and man. When Jesus said, while on the Cross, it is finish, He was not speaking of His purpose here on earth. Jesus was telling us that regardless of our sins, we forever have direct access to our Father. The curtain was rent. The sun refused to shine. The earth quaked. Graves opened and humankind rose. The Son of Man washed away all sin past, present, and future. Jesus made it possible for us to seek and receive forgiveness for our wrongdoings. His sacrifice told us that by nature we are sinners but we do not have to live in sin. We know right from wrong. We only have to go to God when we are too weak to do right. Go to God in the Name of Jesus of Nazareth and ask for forgiveness. Jesus has provided Atonement before God for all human kind. He suffered greatly to do so. He was beaten nearly beyond recognition. Jesus gave His life for you because He knew how important you are to God.

# LIFE WITHOUT WATER

7 1% of the earth is covered with water. A human being can stay alive approximately six days without water. Why did God make it that way? No plants will grow and no animals will remain alive without water. Nothing would live without water. Water in it self is important, however the purity of water is also important. People who do not have clean water to drink will realize major health problems because our kidneys need clean water to wash-a-way impurities. Water is also very important to our digestive system. We recognize the importance of water to our physical lives. However, we seldomly think about the importance of water in our spiritual lives. The Nile River, the River Jordan, the Red Sea. Why was Jesus baptized in the river Jordan? He was without sin. Jesus wanted to set an example to all mankind. After His baptism, a voice came from the heavens saying this is My Son who I love who I am well pleased. John the Baptist told us that when we are baptized in the name of the Father, Son, and Holy Ghost, we have been Baptist with the spirit of God. Our souls have been washed clean. We have stated to God and the world that we have given our lives to God. There are waters and there are spiritual waters. All waters are not the same. Does your soul need to be baptized? You have not lived a perfect life. You have made mistake after mistake. There are so many things you wish you could do over again. It is too bad that youth has to be wasted on the young. We need the purity of spiritual waters to wash-a-way our impurities in life. But then, we have survived. The reason is that our most important decision in life was correct. We accepted God into our lives. Our souls have been baptized. All sins and mistakes have been washed away. We cannot correct the past and we do not have to. God has washed our slant clean. We have only to live today and tomorrow in the light of God. It is a present. Today is the present and the Lord wants you to open your gifts and enjoy His peace and contentment. Your life is in the hands of God.

# TRUST

Can God trust you? Why should God trust you? In order to go to heaven, you must prove to God that you are to be trusted. God is very selective as to who He permits into His kingdom. There are no trial and error considerations. God will permit you to go through hades to determine if you are a correct choice. Only when you feel deep inside that nothing that happens to you here on earth will stop you from loving and trusting in God, will you be acceptable in His sight. We wonder why God permits Satan to continue his evil ways. To continue to lock the gate of heaven to so many. God does not control everything. He has the power to do so, however, God controls only that which has an effect upon His plan and purpose. The devil is a part of God's plan. God wants to know that your belief in Him is so strong that you control the devil. Satan is only as effective as you permit him to be. You have to control your mind. You cannot permit Satan access to your thinking. You are a natural sinner. If you permit your mind to control you, sin will result. You must control your thinking. You must know God's word and use His word to protect you from the devil who will take over your mind if you are weak. You cannot be open minded. Your mind must have rules of entry and enforcement. God's word must determine both entry and enforcement. You must keep your mind stayed on Jesus. If you do not, the devil will make a fool of you. He will lock you out of heaven. He will take away your blessings and Salvation. Satan will make things happen in your life that are designed to make you turn you back on God. Satan wants you to love yourself so much that your love for God is secondary. Your life is a result of what you value. Do you value your life more than you value God? The greatest Commandment is to love God. The second greatest Commandment is to love yourself because you cannot love your neighbor without first love for self. First you must love God with all your heart, mind and strength. When you love God, you love all that God has created. That includes yourself. You must never place love for self above love for God. You must live your life in a manner that tells God you are to be trusted. Your Salvation depends on it. You know death is coming. There is nothing you can do to stop it. You had no control over coming into this world and you will have no control over leaving. The reason is to let us know that God has the final word. Only He makes the final decision. We have no choice. Trust in God and pray that He will have trust in you.

# GOD DIDN'T PROMISE US SUNSHINE

Heaven on earth. When we are born, something was related to us without words. We were led to believe that the purpose of this life is enjoyment, pleasure, and sunshine. As we increased in age and knowledge, we found that enjoyment, pleasure and sunshine was hard to find. We found out about God. First, we learned that we need God to keep from going to hades. Some of us have never discovered that there is more to it than just not going to hades. Sight is a choice. If you don't believe it, just close your eyes. Life is full of choices. You choose to follow Jesus. You choose to learn all that Jesus has done for you. There are those who make the choice not to see. Not to forgive. Not to accept God into their lives. Then there are those who are in it only for themselves. What's in it for me? We can only pray for their increased understanding. It is time to stop hating and start praying. You cannot hate what you pray for. It is time to turn on the lights in our lives. We have been living in darkness too long. Darkness is the absence of light not the other way around. You can't buy a dark blub. You can't turn up the dark. Now is the time for us to start realizing what life is all about. We were not placed here to have fun. God did not promise us sunshine. We were given life to grow in the spirit of God. We were given life to experience the peace and contentment that only God can offer. These are our good times. We don't have to be concerned about the negative feelings of others. No one can curse what God has blessed. We make life difficult simply because of our lack of understanding. When we come to the understanding that the love of God is our true purpose, life becomes manageable. Praising God is fun. Living a life of peace and contentment is a pleasure. Through it all. God, you took my mother, dad, wife, child. When you take me Lord, with my last breath I will praise Your Holy Name.

# YOUTH IS WASTED ON THE YOUNG

Why is it that when you go to church you seldomly see people in their twenties? Why is it that you seldomly hear the name Jesus come out of the mouth of a person between twenty and thirty? Could it be a lack of teaching? Could it be a lack of understanding? Youth are so full of themselves. They think they will live forever. They are so full of life that they fail to see what life is all about. They are young, strong, healthy but not very wise. They do not yet understand that the day will come when they realize you ain't all that. It all will leave them. Youth, strength, health. That's what life will do to you. Make you realize that you ain't all that. Make you realize that how you see your God has a lot to do with how you see yourself. A young preacher stands in front of a congregation that has been going to church more years than he has been alive. His sermon to them is very elementary. They must understand that it takes time to grow in the spirit of God. They must understand that this young man is on the right track. Headed in the right direction. The depth of his sermons will increase as his wisdom increases. As he continues to grow in God's spirit. As he continues to grow from the experiences of life. Is youth wasted on the young? Only if the young fail to learn from their youth. No, I don't enjoy listening to anyone preach a third-grade sermon to a high school class. I'm glad that he is doing it. I'm so glad that young preacher has been visited by the Holy Ghost and pointed in the right direction. When I see young people in church, my heart jumps with joy. I believe in the saying, teach a youth in the ways of God and he/she will not depart from it. They might leave it for awhile, however, they will return to their foundation. They might not even realize it. It is like a magnet continuing to pull you in the right direction. You can't help yourself. That's the spirit of God working in your life. You can't see it but you can feel it and you can't resist. You are a child of God and there is nothing you can do about it. There is nothing you want to do about it other than grow in the spirit of God.

# FEAR

The dictionary tells us that fear is an uneasy feeling that something may happen contrary to one's desires. We have been told that the word fear in the bible means respect. Why is it that the only time the definition of the word fear changes is when it appears in the bible? Human beings have a history of changing God's word to fit their desires. The word respect did exist when the bible was translated. If scripture wanted it to read respect, they would have used the word. They did not. Scripture reads fear of the Lord is the beginning of wisdom. When you were a child, your parents told you to look both ways before crossing the street or you would get your butt spanked. You looked both ways not because you knew what would happen if a car hit you but because you knew what would happen if your mother hit you. Fear of the pain of being spanked. When you grew older, you still looked both ways with more understanding. The fear of the Lord is the beginning of wisdom and knowledge of the Holy One is understanding. When you learned about God, the first thing you learned was that you better be good or you will go to hades. Fear of going to hades always stayed in the back of your mind. As you grew older, fear was accompanied by love, respect, and reverence but it started with fear. Man does not want to thinks that God wants us to fear Him so he changes the word fear to the word respect without reading the word beginning in scripture. Losing fear of God can be dangerous. You can lose many things in life but you will never lose fear because you love yourself. Man has in the past lost fear of the wrath of God. We were given the Ten Commandments because man started to believe that they could do anything without realizing the wrath of the Lord. Sodom and Gomorrah were destroyed primarily because the people lost fear of God. Let all the earth fear the Lord. You are a human being. The devil is after your soul. He will be successful if you stop fearing God. Love and respect might come and go but fear will never leave you. Never stop fearing God.

# TIME

**Y**ou are running out of time. Time is the most important factor in your life. You can get more of anything but time. You can get another house. You can get another car. You cannot get a replacement for today. That is the reason God limited the number of days in your life. You only have a limited amount of time to make the right decisions. The most important things in life take time to acquire. The best food is slow cooked. Wisdom comes only through time because of experiences. Wisdom is more important than a high I.Q.. It takes time to understand that this life is not about you. It takes wisdom to understand that there is something more important in this world than you. Something Higher. Some people suffer from narcissism. Excessive admiration for or fascination with oneself. There will come a time in your life when you will wish you could do something for someone else. When you will wish you could do something for yourself. When you will finally realize you ain't all that. Love of one's self. When you go to church, why is it that the vast majority of people there are up in age? Where are the teenagers and the people in their twenties? They get up five days a week to go to school or work. However, when Sunday morning comes, they say I'm thinking about it. They have not yet acquired the wisdom to understand that there is something higher than themselves that requires attention. They come to that realization only with time. Are you running out of time? That car that you worked long hours to pay for will sooner or later have to be re-placed. Your children will grow-up and leave you. Your health will not always be as good as you would like. You are getting to the place in life where you understand that there has to be something greater than you. Greater than this world. Oh, if you could have only realized this long ago. Think about all of the decisions you made that would have been different. How much farther in this life would you have been if you then had the wisdom you have now? The past is behind you. Your narcissistic ways are behind you. Jesus told the thief on the cross next to him, this day you will be with Me in paradise because the thief had just enough time to set his soul right. You are running out of TIME?

# WHATEVER YOU NEED

Wisdom reminds us of our limitations. The older we get the more we realize that there are more things in this world beyond our control than within our control. Sometimes it does not matter rather we are right or wrong. We still no not have the power to make it happen. We are so glad that God is in control. There are simply too many human beings who are narcissist. They fail to understand that their time is also short. They fail to understand that they are running out of time. That they will end up just like all of us. Face up in the ground. The silly games that people play. Till they are covered up with flowers in the back of a black limousine. Only when they are on their death bed will they realize that it was all meaningless. When they are on their death beds, they will still be thinking about themselves. Fifty years from now, people will not even remember their names because they too will be deceased. Some of these narcissistic people will be forgotten as soon as they are buried. Oh, if they could have only stopped thinking about themselves long enough to give some understanding to their Creator. What you want baby I got it. What you need, you know I got it. All I want is a little respect Before you come home. You can be as mean and disagreeable as you want to be but sooner or later God will see that it all will end. You don't have any excuses. He revealed it all to you in advance. He told you right from wrong. He gave you time to correct your mistakes. He even told you that it will end someday. You can be mule headed if you want to but you will get exactly what you deserve. That's all God wants. A little respect. That is if you want to go home. No, you don't have to go home. But you are going to leave here. There is another place that has been prepared for you. But you will find that it is not cool.

# YOU AND GOD

The opinions of people are very important. What others think of you means a lot. For some people, their reputation is bigger than they are. No good person wants to have a bad reputation. That's the reason you will not tell everything about yourself to anyone. Most people simply do not have the wisdom to handle the truth. Some people get bend out of shape when they hear that someone has said something bad about them. They seem to have an appreciation for the opinions of others to the point that they become upset if the stated opinion is negative. They should ask themselves, does that person have all the facts? Is that person capable of making a rational decision as to the complete person they are talking about? The answer NO will apply to both questions 99% of the time. The opinions of others must always be taken with a grain of salt. There are a high number of people who go through life seeing what is wrong rather than what is right. There are only two sources that have the ability to evaluate the complete picture. That is the reason you should be far more concerned with these two opinions. What you think of yourself and what your God thinks of you. Corrections will have to be made with all of us. No one is perfect. Thank God that He does not require perfection. The more you thank God for what is right the more He will take care of what is wrong. Keep growing in God's spirit. He will fill whatever you will build. You and God. That means more than anything. Everything else is secondary. God is the only source you can turn to in all situations. He is always there for you. Worry is a sign of a lack of faith. You don't have to worry. God won't let you down. Nothing else matters. Just you and God.

# WAIT ON THE LORD

This does not mean that you do nothing but wait. God cannot help you if you are dysfunctional. If you have a lack of spirit. God cannot bless what you do not do. God can only bless positive actions. Ask God for help then do all you can to help yourself. He will fill whatever you build. God is there to help you not carry you. When you have a positive spirit, something deep within, God will give you the strength you need. Being a good person does not mean that you will not have troubles. Jesus was a good person. Slaves in the South were good people. Good people often go through hades. Jesus told us that we will have troubles in this world. But I have overcome the world. By telling us this, Jesus is telling us that we do not have to fight our battles alone. There is nothing standing between your soul and your God. When you show God that you are willing to march into hades for a heavenly cause, God will see that you win the battle. Sometimes our troubles are nothing more than a test. Regardless of what happens to you, you must proof to God that your love for Him is above all. When you reach the point that you can say devil you should have gotten me the first time but it is to late now, you have arrived. Weight on the Lord. Carrying the Cross of Jesus is heavy. God above all. Above death, tornadoes, destruction, floods, cancer. There is nothing that can stop you from loving God. This is earth. We will face battle after battle, but, if we stay true to our glories quest we will win the war. When your personal war here on earth ends, your reward will be greater than you can conceive. Through it all, you have stayed true to God.

# BELIEF/COURAGE

It is all in the mind. That which you believe will direct your life. Have you ever stated to yourself that which you belief? Until it comes out of your mouth, it will not have an effect. Not only does it have to come out of your mouth, it has to be spoken numerous times. You have to convince yourself of your belief. There are numerous things of which we are all afraid. We have what it takes to overcome. You cannot overcome anything until you have the courage to confront it. However, you must first belief in yourself. Only when your belief is deep enough will you have the courage to overcome. Abram had a deep belief in God. He would go wherever God directed without even knowing where he was going. He would take the life of his son only because God told him to do so. He did not have to understand. Belief is more powerful than understanding. God told Moses to take the tail of a snake with his hand. Moses was scared to death but he did it because of his belief in God. Belief is stronger than fear. Numerous people are afraid of dying. They simply do not know what if anything happens after death. Belief in God is stronger than fear. A strong belief has to start with yourself. You have to believe that you are strong enough to overcome. Overcome alcoholism. Overcome addiction. Overcome death. You first have to confront it. I am an alcoholic. I have an addiction to drugs and I want to end it. I have made some mistakes in my life that I cannot seem to get over. I cannot go to sleep without it controlling my mind. I need help. Help is waiting for you to accept it. Your strong belief in God will give you the courage to overcome. First belief that God is in you. Believe that He has the power to strengthen you and help you win your battle. His strength will give you courage to not only confront but to also march into hades for a heavenly cause. Total belief and trust in God. That's what God is all about. Belief, courage and trust. You can believe in yourself because God believes in you.

# WHY PRAY?

Peace be still. The word peace was for His disciples. Numerous times we read Jesus saying ye of little faith. If you want to make Jesus angry, ask Him if He cares. The words be still were for the wild. What kind of man is this that even the winds obey His voice? The answer to this question is not complicated. Jesus is the Son of God. A voice came out of the heavens. This is My Son of whom I am well pleased. There are no questions to be asked. Jesus is the Son of God. We can state many reasons to pray. But then why pray? God already knows our needs and wants. So why pray? Sometimes it is necessary to make the statement, I do not know but Jesus did it. Sometimes that is reason enough. Jesus did it and I believe in Jesus. Nothing can be stronger and more meaningful. Jesus did it. When you believe in someone, you do not always have to have all the answers or understanding. Yes, that's right. Just follow the Leader. That's what Abram did. He followed God's commands out of nothing other than faith. You don't have to proof anything to me. Whatever you tell me to do I will do. The writing is on the wall. You have proven Yourself to me. Nothing else matters. I'm Yours. I believe that God created the heavens and the earth. I believe God created me. I belong to Him. Therefore, He has the right to do with me as He will. Never stop praying. If you believe that God heard you the first time, why do you continue over and over again? Why can't you just pray and walk away? I don't have the answer. All I know is Jesus did it. Over and over He prayed to His Heavenly Father. Oven and over again he stated Father not My will but Your will be done. Not even Jesus had all the answers. Only God knows. I only have to know one thing. I believe in God and Jesus Christ. That is all I need. God and Jesus Christ.

# MANIFESTATION

Plainly apparent to sight or understanding. We humans not only want that which we want but we also want it when we want it. Life does not work that way. We are all enrolled in the school of hard knots. Life is a university. There are ways to learn without as much pain and suffering. A man learns from experiences. But a wise man learns from the experiences of others. The problem, who to trust. There is only one entity to be trusted completely. God does not work within your time table. Scripture tells us that God will answer our prayers. It is believed that God answers prayers immediately. We must understand manifestation. God knows what you need and when it is best for you to have it. The ideal of a thing is different from the reality of a thing. We must be willing to accept God's decisions about that which we need. His decision concerning a positive or negative answer and His decision about manifestation. It is also important to follow the instruction of God. An answer to our prayers is not always an act solely of God. When God gives you instructions, it is for a reason. God told Moses to speak to the rock to draw water. Moses was frustrated. Frustration is a sign of investment. Moses had invested time and effort into the lives of the people of Israel. Moses did not follow the instruction of God. He struck the rock twice. The rock was sematic of Jesus. I am the Rock, the Fortress, the Deliverer. Moses was not permitted to go into the Promised Land because of his frustration. However, the life of Moses was an inspiration to many who followed. God can still use you after your death. We must continue to pray for our needs. Only with the understanding, Thine will Lord not mine be done. We must make a sincere effort to drink from the spiritual rock which is Christ Jesus. Christ has been made plainly apparent to our understanding. The manifestation of Christ is the greatest thing that has ever happened to humanity.

# SLAVERY

We do not know of a period in human history in which human beings did not force their will upon other human beings. Over 2,000 years ago, Hebrews held members of their own ethnic group as slaves. Social stratification. History goes back to 3500 BCE. By the start of the 19$^{th}$ Century, it is believed that up to 75% of humans on the face of this earth were trapped in bondage. European countries were the primary reason. It was not until 1416 that the firs European country put a ban on slave trade. The first enslavement in America was in the year 1508. During that same year, the first African slave was forced to America. Between 1620 and 1700, African slaves in America increased to over 3,000. Between 1700 and 1750, African slavery increased to over 31,000. Slavery is part of human culture. Slavery continues today in the form of human trafficking.

Force is the primary weapon of slavery. However, the desire of slavery is to break the will of the slave. To make the slave stop wanting to live for him/her self and live only for the will of the master. When this happens, the slave has lost all desire to be what God wanted them to be. Yes, one can be beaten into this condition. Beaten down physically and mentally. The Apostle Paul stated that he was a slave of Jesus. No, not by force. By desire. It is possible for one to mentally lose themselves in a cause so worthy that it becomes more important than life itself. Martin L. King Jr. knew he would not live long. He had found something worth dying for. Jesus knew He would not live long. He knew His purpose. He believed His purpose to be more powerful and important than life. It has been said that if a man has not found something worth dying for, he does not deserve to live. There is a long list of people who believed God and Jesus Christ were worth dying for. Ask yourself, do I want to be a slave of Jesus? Do I want to give my all to the Lord? Mind, body and soul.

# SOME GOT IT SOME DON'T GOT IT

Life is like an ice cream cone. If you don't lick it, it will melt away right before your eyes. People crack because of pressure. Pressure is all around you. You cannot let up for one day. If you do not pay the rent, you and your family will end up in the streets. There are children for whom you must care. They do not know their left foot from their right. They require your constant attention seven days a week twenty-four hours a day. Most people do not take vacations. They continue to deal with the pressures of life until they crack. Marriages have troubles because of exterior pressures. The fact is, you cannot depend upon other people. They have their own problems. Some have interest in your welfare but people require sleep. They even sleep during day time hours while on their feet when you might need them the most.

If you cannot afford to get away from the pressure physically, you must find a way to decrease the pressure mentally. Some got it, some don't got it. Give most atheists 40 days to get it together or they will go to hell. You will see what they really believe. That is what life is all about. Choices and consequences. 1 John 5:14-15 tells us that God does hear our prayers. You believe that He heard your prayer yet you continue to pray for the same needs and wants over and over again. Why can you not just pray and walk away? Why can you not just leave it with the Lord? Why can you not trust that God not only heard your prayer but will administer to it when He determines the time to be right? Prayer is not only for God. It is also for you. You pray the second and third times for yourself. Not for God. Prayer makes you feel better. It decreases the pressure. Jesus referred to God as the Comforter. The Comforter cares not only about your physical needs but also about your soul. Who touched Me? You have to have faith that just by touching the hem of His garment the pressures of life will decrease. This life is nothing more than a vapor. Only God will last forever. If you really care about yourself, you will protect your interest by accepting God into your life. You might first accept God out of self-interest but the Holy Spirit will take control of your mind and heart and you will come to realize that your life here on earth is secondary to your love for your Creator. That is all you have to do. Open the door. God will do the rest.

# YOU WILL NEED A JUDAS ISCARIOT IN YOUR LIFE

Why did Jesus make Judas a disciple? Surely Jesus knew that Judas would betray Him. We with less wisdom look at others who are problems in our lives as negatives. When we face a negative in a negative manner the results are negative. When we see a gate in front of us in our lives, it is not there to keep us out. It is there for us to open and pass through. We often wonder why we face difficulties. We have done nothing to deserve these problems. Jesus told us that we will have troubles in this life. Jesus had troubles from the day He was born into this world. From birth, King Herod was trying to kill Him. You think you have problems. We all have problems. There is no way around having them. Of primary importance is how we handle these problems. We think about the problem in a negative manner. When we do, the solution will be negative. Jesus understood His destiny. Do you understand your destiny? Do you understand why you are here on earth? If your primary reason is to draw closer to God, you will not accomplish your purpose by having a good time. Good times do not draw you closer to God. They should but they do not. Hard times draw you closer to God. Hard times are a test. Hard times will test your faith and trust in God. There are somethings that can be produced in struggle that cannot be produced in good times. Jesus selected Judas to be a disciple because He knew that He needed Judas to realize His destiny. He needed Judas to help Him keep His mind straight on God and God's will. You have a problem in front of you. Are you thinking about the problem in a positive or negative way? Could the problem actually be a blessing from God? Could the problem help you grow in the spirit of God? Our problems in life are often caused by other people. It just could be that you are the key to another person's lock. It could be that God is using you to help that person overcome that which she/he could not overcome on their own. When you start looking at your problems in a positive way, you start to find positive answers. When you give yourself to another, time and attention, you will find that you are solving your own problems. Was Judas Iscariot a problem or part of an answer? Every decision we make must be with our destiny in mind. Growth in the spirit of God.

# GOD'S DIVINE PURPOSE

What is your purpose for living? You could say, just to enjoy life but life is not always enjoyable. When it is not enjoyable, are you saying that you have no purpose for living? Jesus told us that we will have hard times in this life. It's a good life to be free and explore the unknown. Till the heart aches and you find you must face them alone. Hard times are an everyday issue for some people. When you see them laughing its to keep from crying. Some people are born into hard times. They know it will never get better. You think you have problems. You are lucky. You have an opportunity to find a way out. For some, there is no way out. Your way out could be through others. It really has nothing to do with money. Even that person living in that big house on a golf course sometimes think he/she is living in hades. Why did God send Jesus to earth? To help people. Numbers are not important. Jesus said that where two or three gather in His name He will be there. Thinking about only yourself and your problems is selfish. Your joy could be in others. It is ok to have feelings but it is not ok when feelings have you. Doing want is right regardless of how you feel. Losing yourself in a cause that helps others. That is all God wants. To help you. That is the reason He sent Jesus to us. That is God's divine purpose. Through good times and bad times, I will always be there for you. To help you overcome. When we stop thinking so much about ourselves and start thinking about other people, we find that our own problems find a solution. There are things we cannot explain. It just happens. It works and I do not know why. Or do I? It works because it is God's divine purpose. You have God given gifts that others do not have but need. God gave you that gift for a purpose. Think about Joseph in scripture. He could not help himself. His God given gift could help Potiphar. Bringing Joseph from jail to the position of controlling everything that happened in Egypt and finding a solution to his own problem. It works. My joy is yours. God's joy is yours.

# SPIRIT

God is Spirit, therefore, nothing can be more important. We worship God in spirit and in truth. We believe in a spirit the physical form of which we will never see. The pure in heart shall see God. We have been told in scripture that we will see the great prophets in heaven. This tells us that we will have a sense of recognition in heaven. It will not be in the human form. The Apostle Paul said that flesh and blood cannot inherit the kingdom of God. Our sense of recognition will not be of human kind. We now have a physical or natural body. This is our only form of recognition. This form of recognition will not remain with us in glory. Jesus first appeared before Mary Magdalene after His Resurrection. She did not realize that was Jesus. She believed He was the gardener. Jesus appeared before His disciples while they were fishing. They did not physically recognize Him. Jesus appeared before Thomas who did not physically recognize him by sight. They all came to know it was Jesus. Jesus had been glorified. He no longer was in a natural body. Jesus was in His glorified body. They came to recognize Him through the voice of the Holy Spirit. When you die, your natural body will be no more. Your glorified body will appear. As with Jesus, they can kill you but they cannot kill the Spirit. The Spirit of God will be with you forever. You will recognize Jesus, the great prophets, your earthly love ones. The pure in heart shall see the Spirit. The Spirit of God. Oh, what a great day it will be. Free at last. Free at last. Thank God Almighty. I'm Free at Last.

# PATIENCE OF GOD

You have done all that you can physically and mentally. A person has to want to change. A person must first accept the fact that the present road is going nowhere. If a better life is to be realized, change has got to come. There are some people who will never come to this realization. It is out of your hands. There is nothing more you can do but pray. Give it to God. Believe it or not, God can also run out of patience. There is a point of no return. Some people cannot be saved because they will not be saved. There are people who believe that if it does not happen on this earth, if it does not happen before their eyes, it will not happen. Then there are those who believe that even the worst of them can be saved. Oh, if it were only true. God told Jeremiah, do not pray for these people because I will not listen. Yes, God had given up completely because the behavior of some people had gone beyond the breaking point. You can go beyond the point of God's patience. As God told Jeremiah, before I formed you in the womb, I knew you. All of their lives I have been trying to bring them into the Potter's House. My efforts of shaping them from clay has marred in My hands. The opportunity given them to be functional in My spirit has failed. I have lost all hope. I have run out of patience. I will not even listen to those who pray for them. They must be destroyed. Some believe for everyone who goes astray someone will come to show the way. Oh, if only this were true. There are some who do not have and will never have the desire to be functional in the spirit of God. They feel very comfortable where they are. Comfort will not be available where they are going. God has given you the desire and power to do that which pleases Him. You hate evil. You hate wrong doing. Your desire in life is to please God. You will never have to be concerned with God running out of patience with you because God directs your life. There are those who have locked God out of their lives. God will not force Himself on you. You have to do your part. You have to open the door and permit Him to come into your heart. You have to believe that nothing can happen to you in this world that will lessen your love for God. Nothing. God is everything to you. Everything.

# SHAME

After all that Jesus as done for humanity, the majority of humanity still does not believe in Him. No one else would voluntary have gone through such pain, suffering, and death for people they have never seen. These are people who do not believe after the fact. They do not believe because they do not want to believe. It is amazing. There were people in the Old Testament born hundreds of years before Jesus came to this world who believed God would grace humanity with a Savior. Isaiah was a great prophet. Numerous times he told of the coming of the Messiah. How could a man who lived 500 years before Jesus know of His coming? The prophet Isaiah told of the birth of Immanuel from a virgin. He stated that Christ would be known to come from Galilee. He stated that the clothing of Christ would be divided up and that lots would be casted after His crucifixion. He stated that Christ would be called Wonderful Counselor and that His crucifixion would shallow up death forever. How could Isaiah know such details 500 years before hand? Here is a man of God who believed even before the birth of Jesus and there are those who will not believe after the fact. Jesus said, he who believe in Me were dead yet shall he live. We Christians must stand strong in our faith or we will not stand at all.

# PURE HEART

The most important things in life are difficult to see. You have two hearts. One can be viewed by sight and one cannot. Which heart is more important? If the one which can be viewed by sight stops pumping blood, you will die. Sooner or later, this is going to happen and there is nothing you can do about it. So really, how important is it? The heart that cannot be viewed will never die. Your soul and spirit are also parts of you that can not be viewed and will always be there. That which is most important is buried deepest by God to protect them. They are too important to be viewed with ease. The spiritual heart, soul, and spirit connect us with God. The spirit controls your heart. Your heart control your behavior. Your behavior will have a meaningful effect upon your soul. Behavior is important. God has destroyed whole cities because of the poor behavior of people. When we are in church, we see different stages of behavior. Some people jump and shout. There is nothing wrong with this. Some people just sit there and pat their foot. Tears of joy. There is nothing wrong with this. You don't have to move your lips for your heart to cry out to God. In fact, lip service is a problem with too many Christians. When your time comes, God will look at your heart not your lips. Man has interest in what he can see. God is interested in that which cannot be seen. God wants to know the kind of person you are inside. That which you are inside will determine your outward appearance. You don't have to say anything. People will know the kind of person you are without a word being spoken. Lord, give me a pure heart so I may serve Thee. Do you want to serve God or is it that you want God to serve you? Deep inside, are you only looking for that which God can do for you? A pure heart is more than that which meets the eye. It is more than words and prayers. Jesus said to go into a closet and pray where no one can see you but God. That is what God wants most from you. An intimate relationship. God is the lover of your soul. Your spiritual heart is the most important entity you have. Forget about this world. Say it, mean it, feel it, believe it. God is all the world to me. A pure heart.

# DARWIN'S THEORY

The life of Charles Darwin was 1809-1882. He believed life was formed from plants and animals. Natural selection. Darwin was wise enough never to attack Christianity as does atheism. He stated, not special creations but as the lineal descendant of some few beings which lived long before. How did the first plant or animal get here? Atheist state that there is no God, yet they cannot answer that question. The bible does not even try to prove that there is a God. It simply starts by stating God created the heavens and the earth. No one, not Charles Darwin nor atheist, can prove that there is no God. Why? Man can prove or disprove almost anything. Why can they not prove or disprove the existence of God? There are certain things that God does not want you to know. When you know something to be true, you have proof. God does no want you to have proof of His existence. Belief is the most powerful word in the English language. God has given you numerous reasons not to believe. Death and destruction by natural causes. Surely a loving God would not permit this to happen. I don't understand it. God does not want you to understand it. God wants you to believe in Him beyond all understanding. You don't know the origin of man. You will never know. Darwin and others can state all the reasoning there is but it is only theory. Not even Jesus knew everything. Only God knows. We can only believe. We believe because we want to believe. We want to believe that there is a Heavenly Father having the power to control all. We want to believe that His love for us is everlasting. We want to believe that there is a place in glory for us once we leave this earth. We believe because we want to believe. Nothing, not theory or atheist, will ever stop us from believing in our Creator. Nothing is stronger than BELIEF.

# COMFORT ZONE

I have dinned sufficient. You say you went a fishin. No, I had a plenty. Oh, you didn't catch any. It makes you feel good to be comfortable. After eating a full meal, you simply do not want any more. Until time passes by and that full feeling goes south. There is a time and place for comfort. Religion is not one of them. There is an old saying, if you don't use it, you will lose it. Man has a desire to feel comfortable in his relationship with God. The last thing man wants is to think that God wants us to fear Him. So, man changes the word fear in scripture to a more comfortable word. What makes you think that God wants you to feel comfortable with Him? You don't feel completely comfortable around your boss at work. When you are comfortable, you are satisfied. You don't want any more. No, I had a plenty. When you feel comfortable in your place with God, you lose your desire to grow in His spirit. It does not matter how many degrees you have. How many degrees did Jesus have? You can never get too knowledgeable to grow in the spirit of God. There are some people who think they know the bible backward and forward. They can quote scripture from memory. When they are in a group, they love to talk. They don't know how to listen. You have heard it before. God gave you two ears and one mouth for a reason. Scripture has one primary purpose, to help people. With some people, everything that comes into their head comes out of their mouth. Are you comfortable in scripture? Is scripture your comfort zone? You have to listen before speaking if you are to help others. Coming out of your comfort zone and using your ears more than your mouth might help you grow in God's spirit. You will never reach your destiny in life without continuing to grow in the spirit of God. Regardless of how much you think you know, there is always more to learn. There are two ways to grow in the spirit of God. Knowledge is important. Knowledge of God can be acquired through other people. Listening and reading. Knowledge must also be received by means of divine revelation. This is the way Jesus served God. The best schools in the world could not relate to Him what God told Him directly. All the bible study you will receive will not relate to you to the degree of divine revelation. Stop talking so much and start listening to God. Come out of your comfort zone of scriptural knowledge and listen to the voice of God. God has something to tell you if you will only listen.

# PAST

I t's over. Let's call it a day. Sorry that it had to end this way. You can't stop thinking about it. Before you go to sleep, certain things keep coming to mind. The fact is, there is nothing you can do about it. It's over physically but is it over mentally? One thing Jesus did for us was to ensure that God would not remember our sins. God is only interested in the kind of person you are now. Some of the things you have done in the past were sinful. Some were simply mistakes. Maybe your biggest mistake was not consulting God before making the decision. Maybe you were too dependent upon your own reasoning or that of others. Either way, God has forgiven you. All that remains is for you to forgive yourself. That may be easier said than done. First, you have to accept the belief that you cannot do it alone. You have to believe in the powers of Jesus Christ through God Almighty. Do you really believe that Jesus died on the Cross to forgive you of all sins? How do you know you really believe? Believing is more than just words coming out of your mouth. Believing starts deep down within and then comes to the surface. Believing not only has an effect on the heart but also on the mind. God knows you did wrong with intent or the use of poor judgment. Because of Jesus, it does not matter. God loves you. God forgave you. You will forgive yourself if you really believe in the powers of Jesus Christ through God Almighty. Rest in Me and I will be worthy of you. There is nothing you can do to undo the past. Stop thinking about what is behind you and start thinking about the future plans God has for your life. The best is yet to come. Give it to God, past, present, and future. He won't let you down.

# ADDICTION

There are many words in the English language that have both positive and negative meanings. When we think of an angel, we think in the positive. A supernatural gift from God. An angel can be a negative. Lucifer was an archangel who wanted to take over the Kingdom of God. We do not like to think about pain. It hurts. But pain can be a positive. Pain can tell you when something is wrong and in need of your attention. Fear is another word we do not like. We do not like being afraid. Fear can actually be a blessing. You do not drive your automobile one hundred miles an hour because of fear. You do not smoke because of fear. Fear of the Lord is the beginning of wisdom. A person is the subject of addiction when that person engages in a behavior for which the effects provide an incentive to pursue the behavior despite consequences. We think of an addiction as a negative. We think about addicts. People who are addicted to drugs or alcohol. People become addicted to many different things. Money, pills, eating, smoking, sex, gambling. These addictions can destroy the life of a person. People who have a drug addiction what to get high. They want to get in a state that will permit them to forget reality. They lose all control of mind and body. The one word that is difficult for them to say is help. This would be a wonderful world if all people got high on Jesus. I want to get high. I want to get high on God. I want to lose all control. Mind and body. I want to become an addict. I want to reach the state of being lost in the love of God and I don't want to find my way out. The love of God is a positive addiction. Inner-peace can only be found in our God.

# THE BURNING BUSH

I will never leave you or forsake you. Trouble is a part of this life. Staying productive is a part of this life. Each individual has been blessed with a special gift from God. Every tree must produce its own fruit. Seeds are generational. We often see the same desires in a child that was in a parent. That child must also have the will to take the desire to a higher level. It is sometimes difficult to understand. He walks just like his grandfather who he has never seen. That health problem seems to run in the family. There is so much in our association with God that we will never understand by reading the bible. Many writings in the bible are difficult to believed. Jonah lived in a big fish three days and three nights. The bible is filled with acts that only God can perform. Why did God present Himself to Moses in the form of a burning bush? How could the bush burn yet not be consumed? God was telling Moses that he was to have trouble in the coming days. Trouble, but have no fear. I have overcome the world. Fire can be serious trouble. But the fact that the bush would not be consumed by the fire also told Moses that the will of God shall conquer all. Thy will be done. Shadrach, Meshach, and Abednego were put into a fiery furnace. They like the bush were not consumed because there was a fourth entity in the furnace with them. When your situation reaches the point of being unbearable, there is an entity with you that can never be consumed. An entity Who will give you strength to out last the storm. You can't see Him but you know He is with you. I will never leave or forsake you. I have overcome the world. Lean on Me when you are not strong. I will give you strength to carry-on. All we have to do is ask for His help. Nothing in this world can stop you for you are a child of God. He is walking beside you every step of the way.

# HEAVENLY FATHER

Now Thy lay me down to sleep. I pray to the Lord my soul to keep. If I should die before I wake, I pray to the Lord my soul to take. Father God, I did not have the wisdom to offer this prayer before going to sleep when I was a child. Now, I do have the wisdom. Each night after my head hits my pillow I pray, if I should die before I wake, I pray to the Lord my soul to take.

Father, there are so many people in this world suffering from a lack of wisdom. Suffering from mental illness. Suffering from an addiction to drugs or alcohol. They want to get so high that they lose all concept of reality. We pray for their welfare. Father, we also have an addiction. We are addicts. We want to get high on You our God. We want to get high on Jesus. We want to lose all concept of reality. We want to get lost in Your love and never find our way out. Praise God. Amen.

# TROUBLE

Trouble don't last always. The same problem will not last always but trouble does last always. Trouble will be with you every year of your life. There is an old saying, if I am not coming out of a storm, I'm going into one. If you are hoping to live life without trouble, you are in for a disappointment. There is no way around it. Mother, dad, wife, husband, child, aunt, uncle all will die. You will be standing there looking into space. Not knowing your left hand from your right. The hardest part is there is nothing you can do about it. There are some problems over which we have some control. Your car stops on you. Your tooth is hurting really bad. We act like these problems are the end of the world. We will not accept the fact that life is trouble. Some Christians think that because they believe in God, life should be a bed of roses. We must come to the understanding that trouble is a meaningful part of life. Believing in God does not eliminate storms in our lives. There will be storm after storm. We must believe that with the help of God, we can out last every storm.

Persecution is a serious form of trouble. Other human beings trying to bring their will on another. Jesus suffered from this kind of trouble. One person receives a sentence of ten years for killing another person while another person gets twenty years for selling drugs. A white police officer walks away free after killing an unarmed black man. It will never change. It was that way when you were born. It will be that way when you die. Accept the fact that you have no control in this world. All you can do is hope it does not happen to you. It could. You are dancing and having a good time when some fool opens fire with an automatic weapon. That is the reason God wants us to get ready and stay ready because we have no control over trouble. You could leave this life at any moment. God has a divine purpose for you both during this life and after this life. Understand that your divine purpose after this life is of primary importance. We must live this life with that understanding.

A preacher once said that Jesus is the main way to God. Was he suggesting that there is another way to God other than Jesus? Jesus stated that no one comes to the Father but by Him. Was Jesus saying that we must believe in Him to be saved? Or, was He simply saying that only He will determine who will enter the kingdom of God? Is Jesus the main or only way to God? Personally, it does not matter. I want to enter the MAIN gate of heaven. Not the side or back door. Jesus is the main way to God. As for me and my house, we will serve the Lord. Jesus is Lord.

# TRYING QUESTIONS II

We all know basically good people. They would never hurt anyone. They go to work every day and take care of their families. They help others when they can. Good people. They also never go to church. You hope they believe in God but you have no way of knowing because you have never heard them say one word about God or Jesus. Will they be saved? Will they go to heaven?

Muslims do not believe in Jesus Christ. Muslims do believe in God. The average Muslim spends more time each day praising God than the average Christian. Down on their knees. Face to the ground. Will they be saved? Will they go to heaven? Or, will they not be saved because they willfully reject Jesus Christ? Will Jews who willfully reject Jesus be saved? Will only those who believe in Jesus Christ be saved?

How we want to be with our love ones when we get to heaven. Will we have a sense of recognition in heaven? How will we be able to recognize people who we know in heaven?

Human beings died before Jesus Christ was born into this world. How were people saved before Jesus?

We want to please God. We want to live a life pleasing to God. Should we live our lives trying to please God?

If you believe God heard you the first time you prayed, why do you pray over and over for the same needs and wants?

God knows all. God already knows your needs and wants before you pray. Why pray? Why are you asking God for something He already knows you need?

You love the Lord. You love your child. If God told you to, would you like Abram take the life of your child as would Abraham? If your answer is no, should you be concerned?

One person steals money. Another person walks into church and kills a dozen people. Is one sin greater than the other? Will God weigh the degree of each sin come judgment day?

You love the Lord. You hate sin. Yet, you continue to do or think that which you know is wrong. Why?

Jesus Christ had to know from the beginning the kind of person that was Judas Iscariot. Why did Jesus make Judas Iscariot a disciple?

The Book of Exodus tells us that a slave is the property of another human being. Does God believe that it is ok for one person to be the slave of another person?

We serve a loving God. Why does our loving God permit hardships that not only seriously hurt but also kill people. Earthquakes, tornadoes, hurricanes, fires, floods?

God commanded that the seventh day of the week shall be the Sabbath Day. What human being had the authority to change a commandment of God?

The bible tells us that Jews were God's chosen people. Why?

Why did God make Himself more obvious in olden days than now?

Why does the bible not state what Jesus Christ looked like?

There were 400 years between the writings of the Old Testament and the New Testament. Why? What happened during this period of time?

Is there a difference between intentional sin and unintentional sin in the eyes of God?

Is there anything greater than faith in God?

There are doctors who can do great things. Can a doctor heal you?

Do evil people have a conscience?

Fear of the Lord is the beginning of wisdom. Does God want us to fear Him?

The bible was written by human hands. Human hands translate the bible into hundreds of different languages. Has mankind had the opportunity to distort the word of God?

Who was Alexander VI and what affect did he have on the bible?

# REACH

Wait on the Lord. God does not work by our time table. He knows when we are ready to accept His blessings. Wait on the Lord could also mean weight on the Lord. God will not help a dysfunctional person. One who is not ready to accept His blessings. One who does not have the will to step forward and try. You must have your head on straight if you want God's help. God will not reach for you. He will give you every opportunity to come to Him. You have to knock if you want the door to open. You have to come to the realization that you need His help. You need God in your life. You are moving but you are not getting anywhere. You seem to be walking in place. The years go by and you are no farther ahead in life than you were in yester year. You are not getting anywhere in life and you don't know why. You are driving fast. You are passing others headed in the same direction. Somehow you know you will never reach your destiny without changing directions. Something is missing. Why are you working so hard to get nowhere? Why are you trying so hard to get something you know you cannot keep? A slave is a person who continues to put forth an effort to obtain something that he will never permanently own. You are too smart for that. Deep within, you know that you will have to give it all back. You know that it is only a lease. You are making payments only for the temporary use of it. There has to be something more to life than this. There has to be a reason for it all. It is time to start reaching for knowledge. It is time to find the answer to the question why. It is time to start reaching for faith in God. It is not a mistake that you are going to die. It is not a mistake that you came into this world with nothing and that you will leave with nothing. You have been given this life to find something. You will find that something only when you reach in the right direction. Wait on the Lord. God is waiting on you. He has granted you a limited amount of time to reach out to Him. Do not let this opportunity to achieve your destiny slip away. God is waiting on you.

# SELF-EXAMINATION

You are a Christian. A voice came to you. It told you to confess. The voice told you that a confession was good for your soul. Revelation, examination, awareness. You never before had this experience. You knew it had to come from God. You knew you had to obey. You started to think about your Christian life. You go to church almost every Sunday. You believe deeply in God. You feel somewhat comfortable in your relationship with the Lord. You try not to do wrong. Why does the Lord want me to examine myself? I believe I am living a good Christian life. My conscience has not told me that anything I have done is that bad. Most Christians are the same way. When they start thinking about their Christian life, they immediately start thinking about that which is good. They feel at easy and comfortable in their relationship with the Lord. What make you think that God wants you to feel comfortable with Him? When you feel comfortable, you do not want more. You are satisfied. You go to church and put money in the offering plate. You think you are doing right. You have never given any thought to the ways you can improve in order to grow in the spirit of God. How you can become a better you. Self-examination is a difficult and dangerous duty. Asking yourself if you are just going through the routine, meaning head knowledge, or do you have a true relationship with God? Honesty without pride. Most people do not want to examine themselves for numerous reasons. They might have low self-esteem. Low self-image. Then again, there are some who are just arrogant. God wants you to overcome that which has overcome you. God wants you to step out of your comfort zone. Step out of your routine and step into a new and higher domination in your relationship with Him. You can only do this by doing away with all self-deception. Asking God to take it away. Anything that is keeping you from enjoying a closer deeper more loving experience with Him. Take it away. You have to help. You have to be honest with yourself. You have to look deep within your heart and character to identify that which must be changed. That which is standing between you and God. Self-examination is not easy. It is a difficult and dangerous duty. A honest heart will be your reward. The pure in heart shall see God.

# RACE

It started in grade school. A race to find out who the smartest kid in the class might be. It continued into your adult life. There are more good people than good jobs. You smile and say hello, but you really want that person's job. That person's position. It has always been that way. A feeling of superiority. That's what the slave owner really wants. I run things. I'm number one. A black man is arrested for murder. He states that he is innocent. His attorney (DL) has questions for the first person called for jury duty. (DL) – Do you believe in God? (J) – Yes. (DL) – Do you believe in Jesus?? (J) Yes. (DL) – What does Jesus look like? Prosecuting Attorney (PA) – Objection. (DL) – A witness must swear on the bible that they will tell the truth. A person serving on the jury should have the same requirement. (Judge) – Over ruled. (DL) – Here are two pictures. Which picture is a picture of Jesus Christ? (J) – I don't know. (DL) – Do you want Jesus Christ to look like you or do you want to look like Jesus Christ? (J) – I don't know. (DL) – You are a liar. Everyone who believes in Jesus want to look like Jesus Christ. This person is unacceptable to the defense in this case to serve on the jury.

Are you a liar? Do you want to look like Jesus Christ? Same skin color. What if Jesus Christ were black? Would it make a difference to you? One reason some people are racist is because it gives them an advantage. One reason some people want to be male is that it gives them an advantage. It helps to put them ahead in the race. In reading the Old Testament, it seems that race was not the main factor. The main factor was superiority. Jews held other Jews as slaves. Superiority is the primary consideration. Looking for something, anything, that will give me the advantage. In this society, the word give is of primary importance. Give it to me. I don't want to work for it. If you don't give it, I will take it. That's life. We are living physically in a world of fools stepping on dreams. We do not have to live mentally under these conditions.

God is the answer. His way of life is different. My ways are not your ways. I don't care what you look like. I don't care about the color of your skin. I don't care about what you did yesterday. I care about one thing. The kind of person you are now. Your superior nature must disappear. This is not a race. Your position in life means nothing to a Me. I want to know what is inside of you. That will tell Me the kind of person you are. That is the only kind of person I want around Me. That is the only kind of person I will invite into My Kingdom. Call it what you will. Pure in heart. Lover of your fellow man. You must understand Me. I am that I am. You must understand that I will not accept seconds. You are so concern about superiority. You will be acceptable to Me only when you accept Me as superior to all.

The race is over.

# WHAT'S IT ALL ABOUT

Is it just for the moment we live? What's it all about when you think it out? Where we meant to take more than we give? Or, were we meant to find love? Before starting anything, we should think about what we want to accomplish. We should think about the final results. What is going to happen if things turn out exactly as I desire? Most of the time, we do not think about the ending. We do some things simply for momentary satisfaction. We go to an amusement park and get on ride after ride just for the momentary satisfaction. Flying through the air with the greatest of ease. When the ride is over, the satisfaction ends. When we are born into this world, we do not have the mental capacity to think about the end. As we grow older, we are so involved in life that we do not think about life. Just do it. I once was invited to dinner by a very lovely elderly couple. When I walked into their home, I saw a nice picture of a very handsome young couple. I almost made a serious mistake. I almost said, oh want a nice picture. Who are they? Have you ever looked at an old picture of yourself and wondered what happened? It happened right before your sees yet you did not see it. Worse than that, you did not plan for it. Our biggest problem is that we wait too long in life to ask ourselves the question what's it all about. If we considered this question in advance, many decisions would have been different. Think about it. Life itself is nothing more than momentary satisfaction. You will not be able to remember half of the years. The momentary satisfaction of holding your child in your arms. The momentary satisfaction of love and happiness on Christmas morning. The momentary satisfaction of thanksgiving dinner with your family. What's it all about? Nothing is permanent. Nothing is forever. Don't let those cherished moments get away. They are the only moments you will remember. Soon, it will be only you and your God.

# JESUS AND SIN AND YOU

We Christians believe that Jesus washed away all sin past, present, and future. Jesus washed away the penalty for all sin. The act of sin remains. A person with an automatic weapon walks into a church and kills twelve people. He has committed a sin. He will not be held accountable for his actions before God because of Jesus. This just does not sound right. But we believe in Jesus, therefore, it has to be right. Scripture tells us that God will punish the unjust. This murderer is most certainly unjust. Certainly, God places value on the way we live our lives. We don't know what to think. It is difficult to understand. It is difficult until you have increased understanding of God. No, this murderer will not walk-a-way unpunished. Yes, because of Jesus, his sins will be forgotten by God. The hate in his heart will not be forgotten. You will not be judged for that which you have done. You will be judged for the reason you did it. God will examine your heart when making His final decision. God wants to know why you did what you did. A person who has a heart filled with the love of God can never commit mass murder. A person with a heart full of the hate of the devil has committed himself to burn in hades. The most important part of your body is your heart. When it stops beating, you die. When you do not believe in God, you die. Yes, Jesus Christ has done a great deal for us. However, there is one thing He cannot do. Give you a pure heart. Jesus can help, but the final decision is up to you. It will not be easy. You have to love all of God's creations not just the people you care about. You cannot do or think that which you want to. God has to control your heart, mind, and body. Your life is no longer yours. You have to give your life to God. This is very difficult for a human being to do. We can only thank God that we do not have to be perfect to go to heaven. In heaven, some will be considered the least of these. But try. Give it all you have. The degree of God's glory you will receive when you get to heaven will depend on it.

# IN CONCLUSION

DESTINY

We all have two reasons for living. Both detail our purpose for living. Our earthly destiny. Why we were given this life. We do not consider this question early enough in life. Have you ever asked yourself this question? Sometimes the answer will be revealed to you early in life. The Rev. Dr. Martin L. King Jr. realized his purpose for living early in his life. Moses realized his purpose late in life. Jesus knew His purpose from the beginning of life. These were people fully engaged in their purpose. Their purpose came to them. Such is not the case with most people. Most people live life just to be alive. Until one day it hits them. Why am I here? I know that I am not going to be here forever. I know that all I worked for will someday be taken away from me. I know that I am going to grow older and will be unable to function as I have in the past. There has to be more to life than is on the surface. Why connects to purpose and purpose connects to destiny. It is sometimes difficult to find our purpose for living until we consider the word FOREVER. Nothing in this life is forever. There is a spiritual inclination in you. The point where your present life meets your future life. The point where your earthly purpose for living meets your spiritual purpose for living. The point of realization, this is authentically me.

Authentically. Not everyone has this purpose for living. This purpose must have a beginning and an ending. Our earthly destiny will one day connect to our spiritual destiny. Every earthly destiny is designed to help someone. That's the connection. Your spiritual destiny is designed to help you. Jesus said to the thief on the cross next to Him, this day you will be with Me in paradise. This tells us that upon leaving this life our spirit will be immediately taken to God's Kingdom or to a lesser place. When you attend a funeral, the person of honor in not there. The soul which contains the Spirit of God has returned to the Father. Why are you crying? That person did not first belong to you. That person first belonged to God. You are crying because you have lost a loving relationship. You are crying for yourself. My earthly destiny was only the beginning of my spiritual destiny. It was my destiny to stand behind Jesus, the Son of the Living God, all the days of my life and I shall dwell in the house of the Lord FOREVER.

# REMEMBER

It's a fearful thing to fall into the hands of the Lord
The peace of this world is not sustaining
God is not a score keeper
Christianity is the only faith that has a Savior
With understanding comes wisdom
God wants to turn your need into feed
There cannot be a miracle unless there is a need
Experts made the Titanic. Amateurs made the Ark
A little bit of Jesus applied to a big mess does not work
Prayer without faith is just wishful thinking
All prayer and no work won't work
God will fill whatever you build
It could be that you are the key to another person's lock
You made a mistake but you are not a mistake
If you are the smartest person in the room, you are in the wrong room
Action without faith is dangerous
You have no proof that there is a God because God does not want you to have proof
Christianity is what one wants it to be
Religion is a return to bondage
We worship only God
God can still use you after your death
It is ok to have feelings but it is not ok if feelings have you
You don't have to move your lips for your heart to cry out to God
Self-examination is a difficult and dangerous duty
The ideal of a thing is different from the reality of a thing
An answer to your prayer is not always an act solely of God
Faith is the difference between where you are now and where you want to be
You ain't all that
We cannot change God's word to fit the person
You cannot hate what you pray for
No one can curse what God has blessed
The more you thank God for what is right, the more He will take care of what is wrong

We are not sinners because we sin. We sin because we are sinners

Sin is sweet to the mouth but bitter to the stomach

Love gives itself away

The devil is a part of God's plan

We are saved because of what Jesus did for us not what we do for Jesus

If your primary relationship with Jesus is through the church, you do not have a personal relationship with God

We are not saved because we follow the Commandments. We follow the Commandments because we are saved

MAY GOD BLESS YOU REAL GOOD

Printed in the United States
By Bookmasters